MENTAL EXERCISE FOR DOGS

Stimulate the Mind, Strengthen the Bond. The Complete Guide to Connecting with Your Dog Through Fun Brain Games that Enhance Intelligence and Promote Well-being

Trudi Richardson

Copyright © 2023 Trudi Richardson – All rights reserved.

The content contained within this book may not be reproduced, duplicated or transmitted without direct written permission from the author or the publisher.

Under no circumstances will any blame or legal responsibility be held against the publisher, or author, for any damages, reparation, or monetary loss due to the information contained within this book. Either directly or indirectly.

Legal Notice:
This book is copyright protected. This book is only for personal use. You cannot amend, distribute, sell, use, quote or paraphrase any part, or the content within this book, without the consent of the author or publisher.

Disclaimer Notice:
Please note the information contained within this document is for educational and entertainment purposes only. All effort has been executed to present accurate, up to date, and reliable, complete information. No warranties of any kind are declared or implied. Readers acknowledge that the author is not engaging in the rendering of legal, financial, medical or professional advice. The content within this book has been derived from various sources. Please consult a licensed professional before attempting any techniques outlined in this book.

By reading this document, the reader agrees that under no circumstances is the author responsible for any losses, direct or indirect, which are incurred as a result of the use of information contained within this document, including, but not limited to errors, omissions, or inaccuracies.

Table of Contents

INTRODUCTION 7

UNDERSTANDING MENTAL EXERCISE FOR DOGS 9
- THE IMPORTANCE OF MENTAL STIMULATION 9
- HOW MENTAL EXERCISE BENEFITS DOGS 11
- RECOGNIZING SIGNS OF MENTAL FATIGUE 13

BUILDING A STRONG FOUNDATION 17
- SOCIALIZATION AND TRAINING BASICS 17
  - *SOCIALIZATION* *17*
  - *TRAINING BASICS* *21*
- ESTABLISHING A BOND WITH YOUR DOG 31
- DEVELOPING FOCUS AND ATTENTION 35

MENTAL EXERCISE FOR DIFFERENT DOG BREEDS 39
- TOY AND SMALL BREEDS 39
- MEDIUM AND LARGE BREEDS 40
- WORKING AND SPORTING BREEDS 42
- SENIOR DOGS AND SPECIAL CONSIDERATIONS 43

MAINTAINING MENTAL WELLNESS 45
- MENTAL EXERCISE AS A DAILY ROUTINE 45
- COMBATING BOREDOM AND SEPARATION ANXIETY 48
  - *UNDERSTANDING BOREDOM* *48*
  - *ADDRESSING SEPARATION ANXIETY* *56*
- CALMING AND RELAXATION TECHNIQUES 60
- MONITORING AND ADAPTING MENTAL EXERCISE 66

INDOOR GAMES AND TRAINING EXERCISES 73
- HIDE AND SEEK 73
- TUG OF WAR 73
- DIY AGILITY COURSE 74
- FOOD DISPENSING TOYS 74
- NAME THAT TOY 75
- SCENT WORK 75

FLIRT POLE PLAY 76
BODY AWARENESS EXERCISES 76
MUFFIN TIN GAME 77
SHELL GAME 77
SOCK PUPPETS 78
PUZZLE TOYS AND TREAT DISPENSERS 79
SIMON SAYS 79
FIND YOUR TOY 80
TOY CLEAN-UP 80
BALLOON CHASE 81
PUZZLES WITH BOXES 81
LASER POINTER FUN 82
OBSTACLE COURSE 82
BUBBLE CHASING 83
FIND IT 83
CUP GAME 84
SOCK TUG-OF-WAR 84
STAIRCASE WORKOUT 85
TUG AND FETCH COMBO 86
SOCK BASKETBALL 86
STUFFED KONG CHALLENGE 87
NEWSPAPER SCAVENGER HUNT 87
SOCK PUPPET SHOW 88
SHAPE SORTING 88
CUPCAKE TIN PUZZLE 89
MIRROR PLAY 89
MUSICAL MATS 90
TUNNEL CRAWL 91
NAME THAT SOUND 91
TARGET TRAINING 92
PLAYING WITH CHILDREN 92
INDOOR FETCH 93
FIND THE TREAT 93
MUSICAL CHAIRS 94
BALLOON VOLLEYBALL 94
COPYCAT 95
STATUES 96
RING TOSS 96
PAW PAINTING 97
SNACK TOSS 97
NAMETHAT TOY 98

- DOGGIE BOWLING 99
- CLEAN-UP RACE 99
- DOGGIE FASHION SHOW 99
- BUBBLE WRAP PARTY 100

OUTDOOR GAMES AND TRAINING EXERCISES 101

- FETCH 101
- FRISBEE 101
- SWIMMING 102
- TREASURE HUNT 102
- BIKE RIDING 103
- DOGGY PARKOUR 104
- DOGGY SOCCER 104
- AGILITY TUNNEL 105
- DOGGY OBEDIENCE COURSE 105
- WATER HOSE PLAY 106
- BUBBLE WRAP STOMP 106
- SCENT WORK TRAIL 107
- DOGGY FREESTYLE DANCE 107
- CHASE AND RECALL 108
- FLYBALL 108
- NATURE SCAVENGER HUNT 109
- WATER RETRIEVE 109
- TRACKING 110
- JUMPING THROUGH HOOPS 110
- DOGGY SOCCER GOALKEEPING 111
- CANINE DISC GOLF 111
- LONG-DISTANCE WALKS 112
- DOGGY BOOT CAMP 113
- SCENT DETECTION GAMES 113
- FREESTYLE RUNNING 114
- WATER SPRAY TUNNEL 114
- BICYCLE JORING 115
- DIGGING PIT 116
- FRISBEE GOLF 116
- DOCK DIVING 117
- CANINE FREESTYLE 117
- SNIFF AND SEARCH 118
- DOGGY FITNESS CIRCUIT 118
- DOGGY LURE COURSE 119
- SOCCER DRIBBLING CHALLENGE 119

DOGGY LIMBO 120
TUG AND GO 121
DOGGY OBSTACLE DASH 121
FETCH AND HIDE 122
DOGGY TUNNEL RACE 122
BOUNDARY TRAINING 123
DOGGY BASKETBALL 123
DOGGY TRAMPOLINE 124
FOLLOW THE LEADER 124
CANINE RELAY RACE 125

MENTAL STIMULATION FOR A DOG ALONE AT HOME 127
SNIFF AND SEEK 127
INTERACTIVE FOOD TOYS 127
TREAT-DISPENSING PUZZLE TOYS 128
FROZEN TREATS 128
DIY SNUFFLE MAT 129
BRAIN GAMES 129
PUZZLE TREAT TOYS 130
BOBBING FOR TREATS 130
TIDY-UP TIME 131
SOUND PUZZLE 132
BALLOON FUN 132
BOX TOWER 133
TOY SHUFFLE 133
SCENTED BOTTLE 134
TOY PUZZLE TOWER 134

CONCLUSION 137

INTRODUCTION

Welcome to the wonderful world of mental stimulation for dogs! This comprehensive guide is designed to highlight the importance of mental exercises in keeping our furry friends happy, engaged, and mentally sharp. Dogs, much like humans, possess cognitive abilities that thrive when challenged and nurtured. By providing them with appropriate mental exercises, we can significantly enhance their overall well-being and quality of life.

Throughout history, the partnership between humans and dogs has evolved from their roles as working companions to beloved family members. As our understanding of canine behavior and cognition has deepened, we have come to realize that physical exercise alone is not sufficient to fulfill their needs. Dogs require mental stimulation to satisfy their natural instincts and maintain a healthy mental state.

In this book, we will embark on a captivating journey into the world of mental exercises for dogs. We will explore a wide range of activities, games, and techniques that tap into their innate abilities, challenging their minds and keeping them mentally stimulated. By engaging their cognitive faculties, we can provide them with the mental enrichment they crave. We understand that not all mental stimulation can take place outdoors, so we have included both indoor and outdoor games to accommodate different settings and circumstances.

For those cozy days spent indoors, we will delve into a range of interactive games and activities that can be enjoyed within the comfort of your home. These games will stimulate your dog's mind, keeping them engaged and mentally sharp. From hide-and-seek games to obedience training exercises, we will provide you with an assortment of options to choose from.

Additionally, we recognize that there may be times when your dog needs mental stimulation while being alone at home. To address this, we have included games and strategies specifically designed for independent play. These activities will encourage your dog to think and problem-solve, even when they are on their own. From treat-dispensing puzzles to interactive toys, we will guide you on how to create an enriching environment for your dog, even in your absence.

Moreover, we will explore a variety of outdoor games and activities that take advantage of open spaces, such as parks or your backyard. Outdoor play not only provides physical exercise but also offers ample opportunities for mental stimulation. We will cover games like fetch variations that incorporate problem-solving elements, obstacle courses that challenge your dog's cognitive abilities, and interactive play with other dogs to promote social and mental engagement.

By including both indoor and outdoor games, as well as games for dogs alone at home, this book aims to cater to different scenarios and ensure that you have a diverse range of mental exercises at your disposal. Whether you're looking for activities to enjoy together or ways to keep your dog mentally stimulated while you're away, this guide has you covered.

Remember, mental stimulation is a vital aspect of your dog's well-being, and by incorporating these games and exercises into their routine, you can provide them with the mental enrichment they need to lead happy, fulfilled lives.

UNDERSTANDING MENTAL EXERCISE FOR DOGS

THE IMPORTANCE OF MENTAL STIMULATION

Mental stimulation is a vital aspect of a dog's overall well-being and quality of life. Dogs have complex cognitive abilities and a need for mental engagement to stay happy and healthy. Providing regular mental stimulation for your furry companion is crucial to prevent boredom, alleviate stress, and promote cognitive development. In this section, we will examine the significance of mental stimulation for canines and delve into different approaches to integrate it into their everyday schedule.

Cognitive Development: Mental stimulation plays a vital role in the cognitive development of dogs. Similar to humans, dogs have an innate curiosity and intelligence that needs to be nurtured. Engaging their minds through various activities and puzzles helps promote their problem-solving skills, memory, and learning abilities. Dogs that receive regular mental stimulation tend to be more alert, adaptable, and quick to learn new commands or tricks. By challenging their minds, we can enhance their cognitive abilities, allowing them to better understand and navigate the world around them.

Preventing Boredom and Destructive Behavior: Dogs are social animals that thrive on companionship and mental engagement. Without proper mental stimulation, dogs can easily become bored, which can lead to a range of behavioral issues. When dogs are left unstimulated for long periods, they may resort to destructive behaviors like chewing furniture, digging holes in the yard, or excessive barking. These behaviors are often signs of frustration, anxiety, or an attempt to alleviate boredom. By providing mental stimulation, we can keep our dogs engaged and prevent such destructive behaviors from occurring.

Alleviating Stress and Anxiety: Just like us, humans, dogs can experience stress and anxiety. Factors such as separation anxiety, loud noises, or changes in their environment can cause emotional distress in dogs. Mental stimulation acts as a natural stress reliever by redirecting their focus and energy towards engaging activities. When dogs are mentally stimulated, they are less likely to dwell on their worries and become anxious. Puzzles, interactive toys, and training sessions can provide a healthy outlet for their energy and help alleviate stress and anxiety.

Bonding and Socialization: Engaging in mental stimulation activities with your dog can reinforce the bond amongst you and your furry companion. Participating in interactive games, training sessions, or problem-solving tasks together builds trust and enhances the communication between you and your dog. These activities also provide an opportunity for positive reinforcement and reward-based training, further reinforcing the bond and building a stronger relationship. Mental stimulation is also crucial for proper socialization, as it exposes dogs to new experiences, environments, and interactions, making them more confident and adaptable in various social settings.

Physical Health and Overall Well-being: While mental stimulation primarily focuses on cognitive development, it also has significant impacts on a dog's physical health and overall well-being. Many mental stimulation activities involve physical exercise, such as interactive play or puzzle-solving games that require movement. These activities promote physical fitness, muscle coordination, and weight management in dogs. Additionally, mental stimulation helps keep their minds active and engaged, reducing the risk of cognitive decline and age-related issues, such as canine cognitive dysfunction.

HOW MENTAL EXERCISE BENEFITS DOGS

Mental exercise is just as important for dogs as physical exercise. While physical activity helps keep their bodies fit, mental stimulation keeps their minds sharp and engaged. Dogs are intelligent creatures with complex cognitive abilities, and providing mental exercise is vital for their overall well-being. Here, we will discuss the various ways in which mental exercise benefits dogs.

Behavior Modification: One of the key benefits of mental exercise for dogs is its impact on their behavior. Mental stimulation helps redirect a dog's energy into productive and engaging activities, reducing the likelihood of destructive behaviors caused by boredom or excess energy. By providing mental challenges and enrichment, dogs are less likely to engage in undesirable behaviors like excessive barking, chewing, or digging. Engaging their minds keeps them occupied and satisfied, promoting a calmer and more balanced state of mind.

Learning Capacity and Problem-Solving Skills: Mental exercise significantly enhances a dog's learning capacity and problem-solving skills. Dogs that regularly participate in mentally stimulating activities develop improved cognitive abilities, memory, and focus. Interactive toys, puzzles, and training sessions require dogs to think critically and find solutions to challenges. As they engage in these activities, dogs become more adept at understanding and responding to cues and commands, making training sessions more effective and efficient. Mental exercise also promotes independent thinking and problem-solving abilities, enabling dogs to navigate and adapt to new situations with ease.

Emotional Well-being and Stress Reduction: Mental exercise plays an important role in the emotional well-being of dogs by reducing stress and anxiety. Dogs, like humans, can experience emotional distress due to various factors, including separation anxiety, fear, or changes in their environment. Engaging their minds in mentally stimulating activities helps redirect their focus and energy away from negative emotions, providing them with a healthy outlet for their energy. This helps alleviate stress and anxiety, promoting a sense of calm and contentment in dogs.

Channeling Excess Energy: Many dogs have boundless energy that needs to be channeled effectively to prevent restlessness or hyperactivity. Physical exercise alone may not always be sufficient to exhaust their energy levels. Mental exercise provides an additional outlet for their energy, keeping them engaged and focused. Engaging in activities that require mental effort, such as scent work, agility training, or obedience trials, not only tire them physically but also exhaust them mentally. A mentally tired dog is often more content and less prone to engaging in destructive or hyperactive behavior.

Enriching the Human-Canine Bond: Engaging in mental exercise activities with dogs strengthens the bond between humans and their canine companions. Participating in interactive games, training sessions, and problem-solving tasks together fosters trust, communication, and mutual understanding. Dogs thrive on the companionship and attention they receive during these activities, enhancing the emotional connection between them and their owners. Mental exercise provides an opportunity for positive reinforcement and rewards, further reinforcing the bond and creating a positive association between dogs and their humans.

Slowing Cognitive Decline in Senior Dogs: Mental exercise is particularly beneficial for senior dogs as it helps slow down cognitive decline and age-related issues. Like humans, dogs can experience cognitive decline, leading to symptoms similar to dementia in humans. Regular mental stimulation can delay the onset and progression of cognitive dysfunction in senior dogs. Engaging their minds through puzzles, interactive toys, and training sessions helps keep their cognitive abilities sharp and promotes mental acuity. Mental exercise also provides mental and sensory stimulation, preventing the deterioration of their cognitive functions.

RECOGNIZING SIGNS OF MENTAL FATIGUE

Similar to humans, dogs have a limited capacity for mental exertion. When they are exposed to excessive mental stimulation or engaged in intense cognitive activities for extended periods, their brains can become fatigued. Mental fatigue in dogs occurs when their cognitive resources are depleted, leading to a decline in mental performance and overall well-being. It is important to note that mental fatigue is different from physical fatigue, as it specifically relates to the exhaustion of mental faculties.

SIGNS OF MENTAL FATIGUE IN DOGS

Decreased Interest or Engagement: One of the primary signs of mental fatigue in dogs is a noticeable decrease in interest or engagement in activities that would typically excite them. They may show disinterest in their favorite toys, become unresponsive to commands or cues, or exhibit a lack of enthusiasm during training sessions. Dogs experiencing mental fatigue may seem withdrawn or distant, showing reduced curiosity and willingness to explore their surroundings.

Reduced Problem-Solving Abilities: Mental fatigue can impair a dog's problem-solving abilities. They may struggle to perform tasks or solve puzzles that they previously mastered. Dogs may appear confused or exhibit signs of frustration when faced with mentally challenging situations. They may take longer to process information or make decisions, demonstrating a decline in their cognitive functioning.

Increased Irritability or Restlessness: When dogs are mentally fatigued, they may exhibit signs of increased irritability or restlessness. They may become easily agitated, show signs of impatience, or display heightened reactivity to stimuli in their environment. Dogs may exhibit more frequent barking, pacing, or repetitive behaviors as a result of their mental exhaustion.

Decreased Appetite: Mental fatigue can also impact a dog's appetite. They may show a decreased interest in food or have difficulty finishing their meals. The exhaustion of cognitive resources can affect their overall motivation and drive, including their desire to eat. It is important to monitor changes in eating patterns as a potential indicator of mental fatigue.

Changes in Sleep Patterns: Dogs experiencing mental fatigue may exhibit changes in their sleep patterns. They may have difficulty falling asleep or staying asleep, leading to disrupted sleep patterns. Conversely, some dogs may sleep excessively as a way to cope with mental exhaustion. Paying attention to any significant changes in their sleep behaviors can provide insight into their mental well-being.

Decreased Performance in Training: Mental fatigue can impact a dog's ability to learn and retain information during training sessions. They may struggle to follow commands they previously learned or have difficulty focusing and concentrating during training exercises. Dogs may become easily distracted or display signs of disorientation, indicating a decline in their mental performance.

Increased Sensitivity to Stimuli: When dogs are mentally fatigued, they may exhibit heightened sensitivity to environmental stimuli. They may become more reactive to sounds, sights, or physical contact that would typically not bother them. Dogs may startle easily or display signs of anxiety or fearfulness in response to stimuli that they would normally handle with ease.

Recognizing signs of mental fatigue in dogs is essential for their overall well-being. Mental exhaustion can impact a dog's cognitive functioning, behavior, and overall quality of life. By being aware of the signs, we can take appropriate measures to alleviate mental fatigue and provide our furry companions with the necessary rest and mental stimulation they require. If you notice any of the signs mentioned, it is important to reduce mental exertion, provide ample rest, and engage in activities that promote relaxation and rejuvenation. A balanced approach to mental stimulation and rest will help ensure the well-being and cognitive health of our beloved dogs.

BUILDING A STRONG FOUNDATION

SOCIALIZATION AND TRAINING BASICS

Socialization and training are essential components of a dog's development, shaping their behavior, and ensuring they become well-rounded and obedient companions. Let's delve into the basics of socialization and training.

SOCIALIZATION

Socialization involves exposing your dog to a wide range of people, animals, environments, and situations, allowing them to become comfortable and adaptable in various settings. Socialization should begin early in a puppy's life, but it can also be beneficial for adult dogs that may have missed out on early socialization experiences. In this section, we will discuss the importance of socialization, the critical periods of socialization, and provide practical tips for effectively socializing your dog.

Why is Socialization Important for Dogs?

Socialization plays a vital role in a dog's general health and behavior. Here are some reasons why socialization is crucial:

- Confidence and Adaptability: Proper socialization helps dogs develop confidence and adaptability in different environments. It allows them to feel comfortable and secure in various situations, reducing the likelihood of fear, anxiety, or aggression.

- Positive Interactions: Socialization provides opportunities for dogs to have positive interactions with other animals, people, and their surroundings. These positive experiences build trust, promote friendly behavior, and help prevent behavioral issues that may arise from fear or lack of exposure.

- Reduced Fear and Anxiety: Dogs that are well-socialized are less likely to develop fear or anxiety in unfamiliar situations. They learn to cope with new experiences and are better equipped to handle changes in their environment.

- Better Communication Skills: Socialization helps dogs learn appropriate communication skills, such as reading body language and responding appropriately to cues from other dogs and humans. This promotes better social interactions and reduces the likelihood of misunderstandings or conflicts.

- Improved Training: Socialized dogs are often more receptive to training. They have a foundation of positive experiences, making it easier for them to focus, learn new commands, and respond to their owners' instructions.

Critical Periods of Socialization in Dogs

During a dog's early development, there are critical periods where they are particularly receptive to socialization. These periods are crucial for shaping their behavior and responses to various stimuli. The primary critical periods for socialization in dogs are as follows:

The Socialization Period (3 to 14 Weeks): This is the most important period for socialization in puppies. During this time, they are open to learning and experiencing new things. Introduce your puppy to a wide range of people, animals, sounds, surfaces, and environments in a positive and controlled manner. This period sets the foundation for their future social behavior.

The Fear-Impact Period (8 to 11 Weeks): During this period, puppies may become more cautious and sensitive to scary or traumatic experiences. It's crucial to avoid negative encounters and focus on positive and gentle exposure to build their confidence.

The Juvenile Period (3 to 6 Months): This period marks a continuation of the socialization process. Reinforce positive experiences and gradually expose your dog to new environments, people, and animals. Continue training and socialization exercises to solidify their behaviors.

Tips for Effective Socialization

Having gained an understanding of the significance of socialization and the crucial periods, let's now delve into practical suggestions for effectively socializing your dog:

Start Early: Begin socializing your puppy as early as possible, ideally between 3 to 14 weeks of age. However, even if you adopt an older dog, you can still work on socialization and slowly uncover them to new skills.

Gradual Exposure: Introduce your dog to new experiences slowly, starting with controlled and positive interactions. Avoid overwhelming them with too much too soon. Gradually increase the level of difficulty, exposure, and distractions as your dog becomes more comfortable.

Positive Reinforcement: Use treats, toys, praise, and petting to reward your dog for calm and confident behavior during socialization experiences. Positive reinforcement helps create positive associations with new experiences and reinforces desired behavior.

Controlled Interactions: When introducing your dog to other animals or new people, ensure the interactions are supervised and controlled. Choose well-behaved and friendly dogs or animals, and introduce them in neutral territory. Similarly, introduce your dog to new people gradually, allowing them to approach at their own pace.

Expose to Various Environments: Take your dog to different environments, such as parks, beaches, busy streets, pet-friendly stores, and outdoor events. Expose them to various sounds, sights, smells, and textures, allowing them to become familiar with different stimuli.

Ongoing Socialization: Socialization should be an ongoing process throughout your dog's life. Regularly expose them to new experiences, environments, and social interactions to maintain their social skills and prevent regression.

Training and Basic Commands: Combine socialization with basic obedience training. You should teach your dog the fundamental instructions like "sit," "stay," "come," and "leave it." These commands provide structure and guidance during socialization experiences.

Stay Calm and Positive: Dogs are sensitive to their owners' emotions, so it's important to stay calm and positive during socialization exercises. Your dog will pick up on your energy and respond accordingly.

Seek Professional Help if Needed: If you are unsure about how to socialize your dog effectively or if your dog displays signs of fear, aggression, or anxiety, consider seeking guidance from a professional dog trainer or behaviorist. They can provide valuable insights and tailored training plans to address specific issues.

Remember that each dog is unique, and the socialization process may take time and patience. Be mindful of your dog's comfort levels and progress at a pace that suits them. With consistent effort and positive experiences, you can help your dog become a well-socialized and confident companion.

TRAINING BASICS

Training is an essential component of raising a well-behaved and obedient dog. It establishes boundaries, teaches basic commands, and helps foster a positive relationship between you and your canine companion. In this section, we will delve into the fundamentals of dog training.

Equipment Needed

When it comes to equipment for training your dog in mental exercises, there are a few essential items to consider. Here are some equipment recommendations:

- Treats: High-value treats are an important tool for positive reinforcement during training. Choose treats that are small, soft, and easily consumable. Find treats that your dog finds irresistible and use them as rewards for their successful performance during mental exercises.

- Clicker: A clicker is a mini handheld device that makes a distinct clicking sound when pressed. It serves as a marker to signal to your dog that they have done something right and that a reward is coming. Clickers are effective for precise timing and consistent communication during training sessions.

- Target Stick: A target stick is a long, extendable rod with a distinct target at the end, such as a ball or a colorful disk. It helps to guide your dog's focus and movement during training exercises. By teaching your dog to touch or follow the target stick, you can shape their behavior and teach them new commands or tricks.

- Training Leash and Collar/Harness: A sturdy training leash and a well-fitted collar or harness are essential for controlling your dog's movements during training sessions. Choose a leash and collar or harness that are appropriate for your dog's size and breed. Ensure that the equipment is comfortable and does not cause any discomfort or restriction.

- Training Mat or Designated Training Area: Having a designated training area or a training mat helps create a focused environment for your dog. It provides a visual cue that it's time for training and helps to define boundaries for certain exercises. A training mat can be a portable mat specifically designed for training sessions or simply a designated area in your home or yard where you conduct training activities.

- Treat Pouch or Treat Bag: A treat pouch or bag is a convenient accessory to hold your dog's treats during training sessions. It keeps the treats easily accessible, allowing you to reward your dog quickly and efficiently. Look for a treat pouch or bag that is lightweight, durable, and has multiple compartments to hold different types of treats.

- Training Props and Toys: Depending on the specific mental exercises you plan to engage in with your dog, you may need additional training props or toys. This could include puzzle toys, interactive toys, target objects, agility equipment, or specific toys for teaching tricks or commands. Choose toys and props that are safe, engaging, and appropriate for your dog's size and play style.

Right Toys for Your Dog

Choosing the right toys for your dog is essential to provide mental stimulation and keep them entertained. Here are some factors to consider when selecting toys for your furry friend:

- Size and Durability: Choose toys that are appropriate for your dog's size and breed. Ensure that the toys are durable and can withstand your dog's chewing and play habits. For heavy chewers, opt for toys made from sturdy materials such as rubber or nylon.

- Interactive and Puzzle Toys: Interactive toys engage your dog's mind by requiring them to solve a puzzle or perform a task to access treats or rewards. Look for puzzle toys that have compartments, hidden compartments, or treat-dispensing features. These toys challenge your dog's problem-solving abilities and keep them mentally stimulated.

- Squeaky Toys: Squeaky toys can be highly engaging for dogs as they provide auditory feedback and mimic the sounds of prey. Look for squeaky toys that are designed to be safe and durable. Monitor your dog's play with squeaky toys to ensure they do not chew off and swallow any small parts.

- Tug Toys: Tug-of-war toys are great for interactive play and can strengthen the bond between you and your dog. Choose tug toys that are designed to be safe and durable. Ensure that both you and your dog understand the rules of the game and practice good tug toy etiquette to prevent any accidental injuries.

- Plush Toys: Plush toys provide comfort and companionship for dogs that enjoy carrying around or cuddling with soft objects. Look for plush toys that are made with durable stitching and safe materials. Monitor your dog's play to ensure they do not ingest any loose parts or stuffing.

- Chew Toys: Chew toys are essential for dogs that have a strong urge to chew. They can help satisfy their natural chewing instincts and keep their teeth and gums healthy. Choose chew toys that are specifically designed for dogs and are made from safe, non-toxic materials. Avoid toys that are too hard and can potentially damage your dog's teeth.

- Fetch Toys: If your dog enjoys playing fetch, invest in toys that are suitable for outdoor play. Look for balls, frisbees, or throwing toys that are designed for dogs and can withstand outdoor environments. Ensure that the size and weight of the fetch toys are appropriate for your dog's breed and physical abilities.

- Variety: It's important to provide your dog with a variety of toys to keep their interest and prevent boredom. Rotate the toys regularly, so they feel like they have new and exciting options to play with. This also helps to extend the lifespan of the toys and prevent them from becoming too worn out or uninteresting.

Consistency in Training

Consistency is important when it comes to training your dog. Dogs thrive on routine and clear expectations. Here are some tips for maintaining consistency in your training efforts:

- Establish Clear Rules: Set clear rules and expectations for your dog from the beginning. Consistency in what you allow and what you discourage will help your dog understand the desired behaviors.

- Use Consistent Verbal Cues: Choose simple, consistent verbal cues for commands such as "sit," "stay," "come," and "down." Use the same cues consistently to avoid confusion and reinforce your dog's understanding of each command.

- Consistent Rewards and Consequences: Consistently reward your dog for desired behaviors using treats, praise, or play. Similarly, discourage and redirect unwanted behaviors consistently. This helps your dog understand the consequences of their actions and reinforces positive behaviors.

- Regular Training Sessions: Schedule regular training sessions with your dog. Short, focused sessions are more effective than sporadic or lengthy sessions. Aim for multiple short sessions throughout the day to keep training engaging and prevent mental fatigue.

Positive Reinforcement

Positive reinforcement is a highly effective tool in dog training, as it entails rewarding your dog for desired behaviors. This approach encourages them to repeat those behaviors in the future. Here are some key points to consider about positive reinforcement:

- Rewards: Use treats, praise, toys, or other rewards that your dog finds motivating. Choose rewards that are appealing to your dog and use them consistently during training sessions.

- Timing: Deliver the reward immediately after your dog performs the desired behavior. This helps create a clear association between the behavior and the reward.

- Consistency: Be consistent in rewarding your dog for the desired behavior. As your dog becomes proficient in the behavior, it is recommended to gradually decrease the frequency of rewards. However, it is important to continue reinforcing the behavior intermittently to maintain it over time.

- Clicker Training: This is a form of positive reinforcement that utilizes a distinct sound (click) to mark the desired behavior. The clicker serves as a precise marker that signals to your dog that they have performed the behavior correctly, followed by a reward.

Basic Commands

Teaching your dog basic commands establishes a foundation for further training and helps foster communication between you and your dog. Here are a few essential commands to focus on:

Sit: Teach your dog to sit on command by using a treat as a lure. Hold the treat above their nose, then move it back over their head, which encourages them to lower their rear end into a sitting position. As they sit, say "sit" and reward them with the treat. Gradually phase out the lure, using only the verbal command and rewarding with praise and treats.

Stay: Start with your dog in a sitting or standing position. Hold your hand out, palm facing your dog, and say "stay." Take a step back, then return to your dog and reward them for staying in position. To enhance your dog's stay command, it's important to gradually increase both the distance and duration of their stay while consistently reinforcing their success with rewards.

Come: Encourage your dog to come to you by using their name followed by the command "come" in a happy and enthusiastic tone. When they come to you, reward them with praise, treats, or play. Make sure to always reward your dog when they respond to the recall command to reinforce the behavior.

Down: Start with your dog in a sitting position. Hold a treat in your closed hand and lower it to the ground, guiding your dog's nose towards the floor. As they follow the treat, say "down" and reward them when they lie down completely. Gradually phase out the lure, using only the verbal command and rewarding with praise and treats.

Leash Training

Leash training is essential for ensuring safe and enjoyable walks with your dog. Here are some tips to make leash training a positive experience:

- Proper Equipment: Use a well-fitting harness or collar and a sturdy leash suitable for your dog's size and strength. Avoid using retractable leashes, as they provide less control and can encourage pulling.

- Positive Associations: Make the leash a positive association for your dog. Start by introducing the leash indoors, allowing your dog to explore it and rewarding them with treats and praise.

- Gradual Exposure: Attach the leash to your dog's collar or harness and let them drag it around in a controlled environment. This helps them get used to the feeling of being connected to the leash without any tension.

- Walking Technique: When you begin walking with your dog on a leash, use a gentle and relaxed grip. Encourage your dog to walk beside you with treats, rewards, and positive reinforcement. If they pull, stop walking and wait for them to release tension on the leash before continuing.

- Consistency: Be consistent in your expectations and responses during leash training. Encourage your dog to walk calmly beside you by rewarding them for doing so and using treats or changes in direction as redirection techniques if they start to pull.

Patience and Persistence

Training takes time and effort, and it's important to be patient and persistent with your dog. Here are some reminders to keep in mind:

- Set Realistic Expectations: Dogs learn at their own pace, so set realistic expectations and understand that progress may be gradual. Celebrate small victories and focus on positive reinforcement.

- Short and Frequent Sessions: Keep training sessions short and frequent to maintain your dog's focus and prevent them from becoming overwhelmed or bored.

- Stay Positive: Maintain a positive and upbeat attitude during training sessions. Dogs are sensitive to their owner's emotions, so remaining patient and positive will make the experience more enjoyable for both of you.

- Consistency is Key: Stay consistent with your training methods, cues, and expectations. Dogs thrive on routine and clear communication.

- Seek Professional Help if Needed: If you're facing challenges or struggling with specific aspects of training, don't hesitate to seek guidance from a professional dog trainer or behaviorist. They can provide personalized advice and techniques to address your specific needs.

Prioritizing Safety

Ensuring safety is paramount when engaging in mental exercises with your dog. Here are some key considerations to ensure the safety and well-being of your dog during mental exercises:

- Supervision: Always supervise your dog during mental exercises to ensure they are engaging in the activities correctly and safely. This allows you to intervene if any issues or risks arise.

- Breaks and Rest: Dogs, like humans, can get mentally tired. Provide breaks and rest periods during mental exercises to prevent mental fatigue or overexertion.

- Treat Size and Quantity: Use small, bite-sized treats during mental exercises to prevent overfeeding and potential digestive issues. Adjust the quantity of treats given based on your dog's dietary needs.

- Avoid Punishment: Use positive reinforcement techniques, such as treats, praise, and play, to reward and motivate your dog during mental exercises. Avoid using punishment or negative reinforcement, as it can lead to stress or anxiety.

- Gradual Progression: Start with easier mental exercises and gradually increase the difficulty level as your dog becomes more comfortable and proficient. Pushing your dog too quickly or introducing complex tasks too soon can lead to frustration and stress.

- Breaks and Rest: Dogs, like humans, need breaks and rest periods. Pay attention to your dog's behavior and energy levels. If they become tired or show signs of fatigue, allow them to rest and resume the exercises at a later time.

- Size and Materials: Choose appropriate-sized toys, puzzles, or objects for your dog's size and breed. Ensure that any materials used are safe, durable, and non-toxic.

- Remove Hazards: Before starting mental exercises, remove any potential hazards from the environment that could cause harm to your dog. This includes removing small objects that could be swallowed or chewed on, securing loose wires or cords, and ensuring the exercise area is free of any harmful substances or chemicals.

ESTABLISHING A BOND WITH YOUR DOG

Bonding with your dog is an essential aspect of building a strong and lasting relationship. It goes beyond mere companionship and establishes a deep connection built on trust, understanding, and mutual affection. In this section, we will explore various ways to bond with your dog, focusing on activities, communication, and shared experiences that fortify the bond amongst you and your furry friend.

- Quality Time and Attention: One of the most crucial ways to bond with your dog is by spending quality time together. Set aside dedicated time each day to focus solely on your dog. Engage in activities that your dog enjoys, such as going for walks, playing games, or simply cuddling on the couch. The undivided attention and shared experiences will help foster a sense of closeness and strengthen your bond.

- Positive Reinforcement and Rewards: Positive reinforcement is a powerful tool for bonding with your dog. Use treats, praise, and affection to reward your dog for good behavior and desirable actions. This positive feedback creates a positive association with you, reinforces their bond, and encourages them to engage in behaviors that please you. Regularly show your dog that you appreciate their efforts and actions, and they will develop a deeper connection with you.

- Training and Learning Together: Engaging in training sessions with your dog is not only an opportunity to teach them commands and behaviors but also a chance to bond and learn together. The training process requires communication, patience, and teamwork. As you work on training exercises, you establish a stronger connection built on trust, understanding, and cooperation.

- Physical Touch and Affection: Dogs thrive on physical touch and affection from their owners. Regularly petting, cuddling, and grooming your dog provides comfort, reassurance, and a sense of security. Massage your dog gently, scratch their favorite spots, and provide ample belly rubs. Physical touch creates a deep sense of bonding and affection.

- Engaging in Play: Playtime is an excellent opportunity to bond with your dog. Engage in interactive play sessions using toys, balls, or games such as fetch or tug-of-war. Playful interactions not only provide physical exercise but also create joy, laughter, and shared experiences. The mutual enjoyment and connection formed during playtime strengthen the bond between you and your dog.

- Exploring the Great Outdoors: Take your dog on adventures to explore the outdoors together. Whether it's hiking, visiting the beach, or going for a nature walk, these shared experiences create lasting memories and strengthen your bond. Observe your dog's curiosity and joy as they explore new sights, smells, and environments, and be there to provide support and companionship.

- Communication and Active Listening: Building a strong bond with your dog requires effective communication. Learn to understand your dog's body language, vocalizations, and signals to better understand their needs and emotions. Pay attention to their subtle cues and respond appropriately. Active listening and observing your dog's communication helps build trust, deepens your understanding of each other, and strengthens your bond.

- Take Training Beyond Basic Commands: Once your dog has mastered basic commands, consider taking training to the next level. Teach them new tricks, engage in advanced obedience training, or participate in dog sports and activities. The process of learning together deepens the bond and enhances the mutual respect and trust between you and your dog.

- Routine and Consistency: Dogs thrive on routine and consistency. Establish a daily routine for your dog that includes feeding, exercise, training, and playtime. Consistency in your interactions and activities helps your dog feel secure and creates a strong bond based on predictability and stability.

- Mindful and Present Interactions: When you are with your dog, practice being fully present and engaged. Put away distractions such as phones or screens and give your undivided attention to your furry friend. By being mindful and present during your interactions, you demonstrate to your dog that they are important and valued, deepening your bond.

- Respect and Trust: Treat your dog with respect and build their trust. Avoid harsh punishments or negative reinforcement methods. Instead, focus on positive reinforcement, clear communication, and providing a safe and loving environment. Earning your dog's trust through respect and positive interactions strengthens the bond and enhances the quality of your relationship.

- Emotional Connection: Dogs are highly sensitive to emotions and can provide comfort and support during challenging times. Share your emotions with your dog, talk to them, and allow them to provide solace and companionship. The emotional connection that develops between you and your dog strengthens the bond and creates a unique understanding between you.

- Take on New Experiences Together: Introduce your dog to new experiences and environments. Take them to different places, meet new people, and expose them to various stimuli in a controlled and positive manner. Sharing these novel experiences helps build trust, increases their confidence, and strengthens the bond between you.

- Respect Individual Preferences: Every dog is unique, with their own personality, preferences, and boundaries. Respect your dog's individuality and cater to their specific needs and likes. Pay attention to what makes them happy, comfortable, and relaxed, and tailor your interactions and activities accordingly. By respecting their individual preferences, you foster a deeper sense of understanding and connection.

- Unconditional Love and Acceptance: Finally, one of the most significant ways to bond with your dog is through unconditional love and acceptance. Embrace your dog for who they are, flaws and all. Shower them with love, understanding, and compassion. Dogs have an incredible ability to sense love and respond with unwavering loyalty and devotion. By providing a safe and loving environment, you establish a profound bond built on trust, love, and acceptance.

DEVELOPING FOCUS AND ATTENTION

Developing focus and attention in your dog is essential for effective training, communication, and overall behavior. When your dog can pay attention to you and stay focused on tasks, it becomes easier to teach them commands, reinforce positive behaviors, and strengthen your bond. This section will provide strategies and techniques to help develop focus and attention in your dog.

Create a Positive Training Environment: Establish a calm and distraction-free environment for training sessions. Minimize external noises and distractions that could divert your dog's attention. Choose a quiet area in your home or a familiar outdoor space where your dog can focus on you and the training tasks at hand.

Start with Short and Simple Sessions: Begin training sessions with short, focused intervals. Dogs have limited attention spans, especially when learning something new. Keeping the sessions brief and engaging helps maintain their focus and prevents mental fatigue. Gradually increase the duration of training sessions as your dog becomes more adept at focusing for longer periods.

Use Positive Reinforcement: Positive reinforcement is a powerful tool for capturing and maintaining your dog's attention. Reward them with treats, praise, or play for attentive and focused behavior. Make sure to deliver the reward immediately after your dog displays the desired behavior to reinforce the connection between focus and positive outcomes.

Find High-Value Rewards: Identify treats or rewards that your dog finds highly enticing. Experiment with different treats or toys to determine what motivates them the most. Using high-value rewards during training sessions creates extra motivation for your dog to stay focused and attentive.

Use a Marker or Clicker: Incorporate a marker or clicker into your training routine. A marker, such as a specific word or sound, signals to your dog that they have performed the desired behavior correctly. Pair the marker with an immediate reward to reinforce their focus and attention. Clicker training, which involves using a distinct clicking sound as the marker, can also be effective in capturing and reinforcing attentive behavior.

Break Tasks into Smaller Steps: Complex tasks can be overwhelming for dogs, leading to loss of focus. To help your dog stay engaged, break down training tasks into smaller, manageable steps. Gradually progress from one step to the next as your dog becomes comfortable and confident. This approach allows for incremental successes and prevents frustration or boredom.

Use Verbal and Visual Cues: Utilize clear and consistent verbal and visual cues during training sessions. Pair each cue with a specific behavior or command. By using consistent cues, your dog will learn to associate the cue with the desired action, making it easier for them to understand and respond. This promotes focus and attention to your instructions.

Incorporate Mental Stimulation: Mental stimulation exercises can improve your dog's ability to focus and concentrate. Engage them in puzzle toys, scent games, or obedience training that challenges their problem-solving skills. Mental stimulation tires your dog mentally, making them more attentive and receptive to training sessions.

Use Engaging and Interactive Training Techniques: Keep your dog actively engaged during training by using interactive techniques. For example, incorporate games such as hide-and-seek or search and find activities that require your dog to use their senses and focus on finding a hidden treat or toy. Interactive training techniques not only reinforce focus and attention but also make training sessions enjoyable for your dog.

Practice in Different Environments: Gradually expose your dog to different environments and distractions during training. Start with low-distraction areas and gradually increase the level of difficulty. This helps your dog generalize their focus and attention skills, enabling them to stay engaged in various situations and environments.

Incorporate Regular Exercise: Physical exercise plays a significant role in helping your dog focus and pay attention. A tired dog is more likely to be calm and attentive during training sessions. Prioritize regular exercise and provide opportunities for your dog to burn off excess energy through walks, playtime, or other physical activities.

Break Tasks into Repetitive Patterns: Some dogs respond well to repetitive patterns in training exercises. By incorporating consistent patterns or sequences in your training routines, you can help your dog anticipate what comes next and stay focused on the task at hand.

Be Patient and Consistent: Developing focus and attention takes time and patience. Dogs learn at different paces, so be consistent with your training efforts and maintain a positive attitude. Avoid getting frustrated or overwhelmed, as your dog will pick up on your emotions. Celebrate small victories and reinforce positive behaviors consistently.

Gradually Increase Distractions: Gradually expose your dog to distractions while training. Start with minimal distractions and slowly introduce more challenging stimuli, such as other dogs, people, or noises. This helps your dog build resilience and maintain focus even in distracting environments.

MENTAL EXERCISE FOR DIFFERENT DOG BREEDS

Different dog breeds have varying levels of intelligence, energy, and instinctual behaviors, which means they require different types and levels of mental exercise. In this chapter, we will delve into mental exercise recommendations specifically designed for different dog breeds.

TOY AND SMALL BREEDS

Toy and Small Breeds are often intelligent and active, despite their small size. They require mental exercise that stimulates their minds and channels their energy effectively.

Breeds that belong to this category include Chihuahua, Pomeranian, Yorkshire Terrier, Maltese, Shih Tzu, Pug, Cavalier King Charles Spaniel, French Bulldog, Boston Terrier, and Miniature Pinscher.

Here are some mental exercise recommendations for Toy and Small Breed dogs:

- Puzzle Toys: Provide interactive puzzle toys that require problem-solving skills, such as treat-dispensing toys or puzzle feeders. These toys engage their minds and provide a challenge.
- Hide and Seek: Engage your dog in a stimulating activity by strategically hiding treats or toys throughout the

house and motivating them to search for these hidden rewards. This activity taps into their natural scenting abilities and provides mental stimulation.

- Agility and Obstacle Courses: Set up a mini agility course in your backyard or living room using low jumps, tunnels, and weave poles. Teaching your small breed dog to navigate the obstacles helps improve their focus and mental agility.

- Trick Training: Teach your dog new tricks using positive reinforcement techniques. Small breeds are often quick learners and enjoy showing off their skills.

- Nose Work: Engage your dog in scent-based activities like tracking or scent detection. Hide treats or toys and encourage them to find the hidden items using their sense of smell.

- Interactive Play: Engage in interactive play sessions with toys like flirt poles or feather wands. These activities keep your small breed dog mentally engaged and provide an outlet for their energy.

MEDIUM AND LARGE BREEDS

Medium and Large Breed dogs vary widely in terms of energy levels and exercise requirements. Mental exercise is vital for their well-being and can help prevent behavioral problems resulting from boredom.

Breeds that belong to this category include Labrador Retriever, Golden Retriever, German Shepherd, Boxer, Bulldog, Rottweiler, Australian Shepherd, Siberian Husky, Doberman Pinscher, and Border Collie.

Here are some mental exercise recommendations for Medium and Large Breed dogs:

- Obedience Training: Engage in regular obedience training sessions with your dog. Teaching them commands and practicing obedience exercises challenges their minds and strengthens the bond between you.

- Interactive Toys: Provide interactive toys that require problem-solving, such as puzzle toys or treat-dispensing toys. These toys keep your dog mentally stimulated and encourage them to use their problem-solving skills.

- Retrieval Games: Play games that involve retrieving objects, such as fetching a ball or playing Frisbee. This activity provides both mental and physical exercise for your dog.

- Advanced Trick Training: Teach your dog advanced tricks or complex behaviors. This not only stimulates their minds but also helps build their focus, coordination, and communication skills.

- Scent Work: Engage your dog in scent work activities, such as tracking or search and rescue training. These exercises tap into their natural abilities and provide mental stimulation.

- Agility and Canine Sports: Consider enrolling your dog in agility classes or participating in canine sports such as flyball or dock diving. These activities challenge your dog mentally and physically, promoting their overall well-being.

WORKING AND SPORTING BREEDS

Working and Sporting Breed dogs are known for their intelligence, high energy levels, and strong work drive. Mental exercise is crucial for these breeds to keep them engaged and prevent behavioral issues.

Breeds that belong to this category include Border Collie, Australian Shepherd, German Shepherd, Belgian Malinois, Labrador Retriever, Golden Retriever, Rottweiler, Boxer, Siberian Husky, and Doberman Pinscher.

Here are some mental exercise recommendations for Working and Sporting Breed dogs:

- Advanced Training: Engage in advanced training activities that challenge their intelligence and problem-solving abilities. Teach complex commands, obedience exercises, and work on specialized skills related to their breed.

- Job-Based Activities: Assign your dog specific tasks or jobs to do around the house or during walks. For example, they can carry a backpack with supplies or help with chores like picking up objects or fetching items.

- Herding or Retrieving Activities: If your dog has herding or retrieving instincts, engage them in activities that mimic those behaviors. Set up obstacles or use specialized training equipment to simulate their natural instincts.

- Interactive Toys and Treat Dispensers: Provide puzzle toys or treat-dispensing toys that require problem-solving. This keeps their minds occupied and provides an outlet for their energy.

- Scent Work and Tracking: Engage your dog in scent work activities, such as tracking or search and rescue training. These exercises tap into their natural abilities and provide both mental and physical stimulation.

- Regular Exercise: Working and Sporting Breeds require regular physical exercise in addition to mental stimulation. Combine mental and physical exercise by incorporating obedience training, agility, or other canine sports into their routine.

SENIOR DOGS AND SPECIAL CONSIDERATIONS

Senior dogs have different needs and may require mental exercise that is appropriate for their age and physical abilities. Additionally, some dogs may have special considerations due to health conditions or disabilities. Here are some mental exercise recommendations for Senior Dogs and Special Considerations:

- Gentle Training: Engage in gentle and low-impact training activities that suit their physical abilities. Focus on reinforcing basic commands and behaviors to keep their minds active.

- Nose Work: Engage your dog in scent-based activities, such as hiding treats or toys for them to find. This stimulates their sense of smell and provides mental stimulation.

- Interactive Toys: Provide soft or plush toys that can be manipulated easily by older dogs. These toys may have hidden compartments for treats or squeakers to provide sensory stimulation.

- Massage and Gentle Touch: Incorporate massage and gentle touch sessions into your senior dog's routine. This not only provides physical relaxation but also strengthens the bond between you and promotes mental well-being.

- Short and Frequent Mental Exercises: Break mental exercises into shorter sessions throughout the day to prevent mental fatigue. Focus on activities that are enjoyable, comfortable, and appropriate for their age and physical condition.

- Consider Individual Needs: Be mindful of any health conditions or disabilities your dog may have and adapt mental exercises accordingly. Consult with your veterinarian to determine suitable activities for your senior dog's specific needs.

Remember to always consider your dog's individual temperament, energy levels, and preferences when designing mental exercises. It's important to provide mental stimulation that is appropriate and engaging for your dog's specific breed and personality. By incorporating regular mental exercise into their routine, you can help keep your dog mentally sharp, happy, and well-balanced.

MAINTAINING MENTAL WELLNESS

MENTAL EXERCISE AS A DAILY ROUTINE

Incorporating regular mental exercise into their routine helps keep their minds sharp, prevents boredom, and promotes a balanced lifestyle. By providing mental challenges and engaging activities, you can satisfy your dog's natural instincts, strengthen their cognitive abilities, and foster a stronger bond between you and your furry companion. In this section, we will discuss practical steps to effectively incorporate mental exercise into your dog's daily routine, ensuring they receive the mental stimulation they need to thrive and lead a fulfilled life.

Determine your dog's exercise needs: Assess your dog's breed, age, energy level, and individual characteristics to determine their specific mental exercise requirements. Some breeds may need more mental stimulation than others, while older dogs may have different needs than younger ones.

Set aside dedicated time for mental exercise: Allocate a specific time each day for mental exercise. This could be in the morning, afternoon, or evening, depending on your dog's energy levels and schedule. Consistency is key, so aim for a regular routine.

Use mealtime as a mental exercise opportunity: Instead of feeding your dog from a regular food bowl, consider using food puzzle toys or interactive feeders. These require your dog to work for their food, engaging their problem-solving skills and providing mental stimulation during mealtime.

Incorporate training sessions: Use training sessions as a way to provide mental exercise. Work on teaching new commands, practicing obedience exercises, or refining existing skills. Short and focused training sessions throughout the day can help keep your dog mentally engaged.

Rotate toys and puzzles: Keep your dog's toys and puzzles fresh and exciting by rotating them regularly. Introduce new interactive toys, puzzle feeders, or treat-dispensing toys to keep their minds engaged. This prevents boredom and maintains their interest in mental exercises.

Engage in interactive play: Interactive play sessions are not only physically stimulating but also mentally engaging for your dog. Use toys like flirt poles, tug toys, or interactive treat-dispensing toys to provide mental exercise while strengthening the bond between you and your dog.

Incorporate sniffing activities: Dogs have an incredible sense of smell, and engaging their olfactory senses provides mental stimulation. Create scent-based games or hide treats around the house or yard for your dog to find. This taps into their natural instincts and provides a rewarding mental challenge.

Explore new environments: Take your dog on regular walks or outings to new environments. Exposing them to different sights, sounds, and smells provides mental stimulation and broadens their experiences. Letting them explore and sniff around encourages their curiosity and engages their minds.

Teach new tricks or behaviors: Continuously challenge your dog's mind by teaching them new tricks or behaviors. This not only stimulates their mental abilities but also strengthens the bond between you and your dog. Use positive reinforcement techniques to make the learning process enjoyable and rewarding for both of you.

Provide interactive and challenging toys: Invest in interactive toys that require problem-solving, such as puzzle toys, treat-dispensing toys, or hide-and-seek toys. These toys keep your dog mentally engaged and provide a stimulating challenge.

Make use of downtime: Even during quieter moments, you can provide mental stimulation for your dog. For example, you can practice basic obedience commands or ask your dog to perform tricks while waiting for meals or during commercial breaks.

Consider professional enrichment activities: If you're looking for additional mental exercise options, consider enrolling your dog in activities like nose work classes, agility training, or interactive playgroups. These activities provide structured mental stimulation and allow your dog to socialize with other dogs.

Tailor exercises to your dog's breed and personality: Different breeds and individual dogs have varying preferences and strengths. Tailor the mental exercises to suit your dog's specific breed traits and personality. For example, working breeds may benefit from tasks that tap into their herding or retrieving instincts, while scent hounds may enjoy scent work activities.

Stay consistent and adjust as needed: Stick to your dog's mental exercise routine and make adjustments as necessary. Observe how your dog responds to different activities and modify the routine to keep them engaged and challenged.

COMBATING BOREDOM AND SEPARATION ANXIETY

Boredom and separation anxiety are common issues that many dogs face, and they can lead to unwanted behaviors and stress for both the dog and the owner. It's important to address these concerns and provide appropriate mental stimulation and strategies to help your dog cope with boredom and separation.

UNDERSTANDING BOREDOM

Boredom in dogs can result from a lack of mental and physical stimulation. When dogs are not sufficiently engaged, they may resort to behaviors such as excessive barking, destructive chewing, digging, or even self-harm. Recognizing the signs of boredom is the first step in addressing the issue. Some signs of boredom in dogs include restlessness, pacing, excessive licking, attention-seeking behaviors, or engaging in destructive activities.

Boredom is a state of mind characterized by a lack of stimulation or interest in one's surroundings. It can affect both humans and animals, including dogs. Understanding boredom in dogs is crucial for identifying and addressing the underlying causes to prevent behavioral issues and promote their overall well-being. Here are some important points to help you understand boredom in dogs:

Causes of Boredom

Boredom in dogs can arise from a lack of mental and physical stimulation, leading to various behavioral and health issues. Here are some common causes of boredom in dogs:

- Insufficient Exercise: Dogs are active animals that require regular exercise to expend their energy. Without adequate physical activity, dogs can become bored and restless, leading to behavioral problems.

- Lack of Mental Stimulation: Dogs also need mental stimulation to retain their minds involved. Without mental challenges, they can become bored and seek ways to entertain themselves, often resorting to destructive behaviors.

- Lack of Social Interaction: Dogs are social creatures and thrive on social interaction with humans and other animals. Isolation or limited social opportunities can contribute to boredom and loneliness.

- Lack of Environmental Enrichment: An unstimulating environment devoid of toys, interactive puzzles, and sensory experiences can leave dogs feeling bored. Dogs need opportunities to explore and engage with their surroundings.

- Monotonous Routine: Dogs appreciate variety and novelty in their daily lives. A monotonous routine without new experiences or activities can result in boredom.

- Lack of Human Attention: Dogs crave attention and companionship from their human caregivers. If they are left alone for extended periods or receive insufficient attention and interaction, they can become bored and develop behavioral issues.

- Lack of Training and Mental Challenges: Dogs thrive on learning and problem-solving. Without training and mental challenges, they may become bored and frustrated.

- Separation or Changes in Routine: Sudden changes in routine or being separated from their human companions can lead to boredom and anxiety in dogs.

Signs of Boredom in Dogs

Boredom in dogs can manifest in various ways. Here are some common signs that may indicate that your dog is feeling bored:

- Destructive Behavior: Dogs may engage in destructive behaviors, such as chewing furniture, shoes, or other household items, as a way to alleviate their boredom and release pent-up energy.

- Excessive Barking: Boredom can lead to excessive barking, particularly when dogs are seeking attention or stimulation. They may bark persistently or for prolonged periods.

- Restlessness and Pacing: If a dog is bored, they may exhibit restless behavior, pacing back and forth or wandering aimlessly around the house or yard.

- Digging: Dogs may resort to digging holes in the yard or scratching at carpets and furniture when they are bored and seeking a way to entertain themselves.

- Attention-Seeking Behavior: Bored dogs may display attention-seeking behaviors, such as nudging, pawing, or whining, to gain the attention and interaction of their owners.

- Lack of Interest in Toys or Activities: If a dog is bored, they may show disinterest in their usual toys or activities. They may ignore toys, not engage in play, or quickly lose interest in games.

- Excessive Sleeping: While dogs naturally sleep a significant portion of the day, excessive sleeping can indicate boredom. Dogs may sleep more out of lack of stimulation or as a way to pass the time.

- Hyperactivity or Restlessness: Paradoxically, some dogs may become hyperactive or exhibit restless behavior when they are bored. They may display increased energy levels and engage in frenzied behavior.

- Inappropriate Elimination: Boredom can lead to frustration or anxiety, resulting in dogs urinating or defecating inappropriately indoors, even if they are typically house-trained.

- Seeking Attention: Dogs may attempt to seek attention or engage in attention-seeking behaviors when they are bored. They may nudge, paw, or jump on their owners to elicit a response.

Negative Effects of Boredom

Boredom can have negative effects on their overall well-being and behavior. Here are some potential negative consequences of prolonged boredom in dogs:

- Destructive Behavior: Bored dogs may resort to destructive behaviors, such as chewing furniture, shoes, or other household items. This can result in property damage and potential harm to the dog if they ingest harmful objects.

- Behavioral Issues: Boredom can contribute to the development of various behavioral problems, including excessive barking, digging, jumping, and aggression. These behaviors can strain the bond between the dog and their owners and lead to difficulties in training and socialization.

- Anxiety and Stress: Boredom can contribute to increased anxiety and stress levels in dogs. When they are not mentally and physically stimulated, they may become anxious, leading to symptoms such as restlessness, excessive panting, trembling, or destructive behaviors.

- Obesity and Health Issues: Lack of physical exercise and mental stimulation can contribute to weight gain and obesity in dogs. Boredom-induced overeating, coupled with a sedentary lifestyle, can lead to health problems such as diabetes, joint issues, and cardiovascular conditions.

- Escaping or Roaming: Boredom may drive dogs to seek out stimulation or entertainment outside of their home environment. They may attempt to escape yards or homes, leading to potential dangers like traffic accidents or encounters with other animals.

- Reduced Quality of Life: Boredom can significantly impact a dog's quality of life. Without mental and physical stimulation, dogs may experience a lack of fulfillment and engagement, leading to a less enriching and enjoyable existence.

- Relationship Strain: Boredom-related behaviors can strain the relationship between dogs and their owners.

Destructive behaviors, excessive barking, or aggression can cause frustration, stress, and conflict, leading to a breakdown in the human-dog bond.

Ways To Combat Bordeom

Providing Sufficient Exercise : Physical exercise is crucial for dogs to release energy and maintain their overall well-being. Regular exercise sessions help prevent boredom by keeping your dog physically tired and content. Aim for daily walks, runs, or play sessions that are appropriate for your dog's breed, age, and health. Remember that different breeds have different exercise needs, so tailor the activities accordingly. For high-energy breeds, consider engaging in activities such as fetch, agility training, or swimming to provide them with adequate physical exercise.

Mental Stimulation: Mental exercise is equally important as physical exercise for combating boredom. Engage your dog's mind through activities such as puzzle toys, treat-dispensing toys, interactive games, and obedience training. These activities provide mental challenges and help keep your dog mentally stimulated and entertained. Interactive toys, such as puzzle feeders or toys that require problem-solving skills to access treats, are excellent options to engage your dog's mind. These toys encourage them to think, problem-solve, and work for their rewards, which helps alleviate boredom.

Enrichment Toys and Activities: Enrichment toys are designed to engage a dog's senses and provide mental stimulation. Toys like puzzle feeders, Kong toys filled with treats, or interactive toys that dispense food can keep your dog occupied and mentally stimulated. Rotate the toys regularly to maintain their novelty and prevent boredom. You can also create homemade enrichment activities by hiding treats or toys around the house or using items such as cardboard boxes or empty plastic bottles for your dog to explore and interact with.

Interactive Playtime: Engage in interactive play sessions with your dog to provide mental and physical stimulation. Play fetch, tug-of-war, or engage in hide-and-seek games. Interactive play not only helps alleviate boredom but also strengthens the bond between you and your dog. Use toys that encourage active play, such as balls, frisbees, or rope toys, to keep your dog engaged and mentally stimulated during playtime.

Training and Mental Challenges: Regular training sessions provide mental stimulation for dogs. Teach new tricks, practice obedience commands, and engage in scent work or agility training. These activities challenge your dog's mind and provide an outlet for their energy. Incorporate short training sessions throughout the day to keep your dog mentally engaged and to reinforce positive behaviors.

Food Dispensing Toys and Slow Feeders: Using food-dispensing toys or slow feeders can turn mealtime into a mentally stimulating activity. Instead of feeding your dog from a regular bowl, use toys or feeders that require them to work for their food. This engages their problem-solving skills and keeps them mentally engaged while eating. Slow feeders, such as puzzle bowls or interactive feeders, require dogs to navigate obstacles or work around different sections to access their food, which can provide mental stimulation and slow down fast eaters.

Interactive Treat Hunt: Create a fun and mentally stimulating treat hunt for your dog. Hide treats around the house or yard and encourage them to search for them. This taps into their natural scenting abilities and provides mental stimulation. Start with easy hiding spots and gradually increase the difficulty level. You can also use scent-based games or nose work activities to engage their sense of smell and provide mental challenges.

Environmental Enrichment: Create an enriched environment for your dog by providing different textures, sounds, and scents. Provide toys, safe chew items, and sensory experiences such as nature sounds or calming music. This helps keep their minds engaged and prevents boredom. Set up an area where your dog can observe the outside world, such as near a window or a designated outdoor space. Providing visual and auditory stimulation can help keep them entertained and mentally stimulated.

Rotate Toys and Activities: Regularly rotate your dog's toys and activities to keep them mentally stimulated. Introduce new toys, puzzles, or activities and retire others for a while. This prevents boredom from setting in and keeps your dog engaged and excited about their playtime. Keep a selection of toys and rotate them every few days to maintain their novelty. You can also switch up the types of activities you engage in, such as alternating between training sessions, interactive play, and puzzle toy time.

Interactive Dog Puzzles: Invest in interactive dog puzzles that require problem-solving skills. These puzzles have hidden compartments, sliding parts, or movable pieces that your dog needs to figure out to access treats. They provide mental stimulation and keep your dog entertained. Start with simpler puzzles and gradually increase the difficulty level as your dog becomes more proficient. Supervise your dog during puzzle play to ensure their safety and to assist them if they become frustrated.

ADDRESSING SEPARATION ANXIETY

Separation anxiety is a condition where dogs experience excessive distress and anxiety when separated from their owners or when left alone. It can manifest in various ways, such as excessive vocalization, destructive behavior, house soiling, or self-harm.

Causes

Separation anxiety in dogs can have various underlying causes, and it's essential to understand them to effectively address the issue. Below are several typical factors that can contribute to separation anxiety in dogs:

- Early Life Experiences: Dogs that have experienced traumatic events or have been separated from their mothers and littermates at an early age may be more prone to developing separation anxiety. Lack of proper socialization during this critical period can contribute to anxiety-related behaviors when separated from their human caregivers later on.

- Changes in Routine: Dogs are creatures of habit, and sudden changes in their daily routine or environment can trigger anxiety. Events such as moving to a new home, a change in work schedules, or the addition or loss of family members can disrupt their sense of security and contribute to separation anxiety.

- Bonding and Attachment: Dogs are highly social animals and form strong bonds with their human caregivers. Dogs that are overly dependent or have a strong attachment to a specific person may experience anxiety when separated from them. This attachment can be intensified if the dog has experienced past abandonment or neglect.

- Lack of Proper Training: Dogs that have not been adequately trained or conditioned to be alone may struggle with separation anxiety. If a dog has never learned to feel comfortable and secure when left alone, they may become anxious or distressed in such situations.

- Genetics and Breed Predisposition: Some dog breeds, such as Labrador Retrievers, German Shepherds, and Vizslas, may be more susceptible to to separation anxiety due to their genetic predisposition. It's important to note that any dog, regardless of breed, can develop separation anxiety.

- Inconsistent or Negative Experiences: Dogs that have had negative experiences while being alone, such as confinement in a small space for extended periods or punishment associated with being left alone, can develop anxiety and associate those negative experiences with future separations.

- Lack of Mental Stimulation: Dogs require mental stimulation and engaging activities to keep their minds occupied. Boredom and lack of mental stimulation can contribute to anxiety and destructive behaviors when left alone for extended periods.

Strategies

Here are some strategies to help address separation anxiety in dogs:

Gradual Departures and Arrivals

- Practice short departures and gradually increase the duration over time. This helps desensitize your dog to your departure cues and reduces anxiety associated with your absence.

- Keep departures and arrivals low-key. Avoid making a big fuss or showing excessive emotions when leaving or returning home. This helps normalize departures and reduces the stress associated with them.

Establish a Predictable Routine

- Dogs thrive on routine and predictability. Establish a reliable daily routine for your dog, containing regular feeding times, exercise sessions, and rest periods. A predictable routine helps create a sense of security and can reduce anxiety.

Create a Safe and Comfortable Space

- Deliver a chosen safe space for your dog where they can feel secure and comfortable when left alone. This can be a crate, a specific room, or an area with their bed, toys, and familiar scents.

- Gradually acclimate your dog to the safe space by introducing positive associations. Offer treats, toys, or praise when they willingly enter and spend time in their designated space.

Counterconditioning and Desensitization

- Counterconditioning involves changing your dog's emotional response to being alone by pairing it with positive experiences.

- Start by leaving your dog alone for short periods and gradually increase the duration. During these departures, offer special treats or engage your dog in a favorite activity. This helps create positive associations with being alone.

- Use desensitization techniques to gradually expose your dog to departure cues (e.g., picking up keys, putting on shoes) without actually leaving. By repeatedly exposing them to these cues without the associated anxiety of departure, you can help reduce their sensitivity to them.

Interactive Toys and Treats

- Provide interactive toys or treat-dispensing toys that can keep your dog mentally engaged and occupied while you are away. These toys provide a positive distraction and can help alleviate anxiety.

- Fill puzzle toys with treats or use frozen Kong toys to provide long-lasting entertainment and mental stimulation for your dog during your absence.

Calming Strategies

- Explore calming strategies to help reduce anxiety. This can include playing soothing music or leaving the TV on to provide background noise, using pheromone diffusers like Adaptil, or using anxiety wraps or shirts that provide a gentle, calming pressure.

Professional Help

- If your dog's separation anxiety is severe or continues to persist despite your best efforts, it is wise to seek professional assistance from a certified dog trainer or animal behaviorist who specializes in addressing separation anxiety. They can provide specific behavior modification techniques, tailored to your dog's needs, and guide you through the process of addressing separation anxiety effectively.

Medication

- In severe cases of separation anxiety, medication prescribed by a veterinarian may be necessary to help manage the condition. Medication can help reduce anxiety levels and allow behavior modification techniques to be more effective. Consult with a veterinarian or a veterinary behaviorist to discuss the possibility of medication if needed.

CALMING AND RELAXATION TECHNIQUES

Calming and relaxation techniques can be beneficial for dogs in various situations, including during times of stress, anxiety, or hyperactivity. These techniques help promote a sense of calmness, reduce anxiety, and create a more relaxed state of mind for your dog. Here are some effective calming and relaxation techniques for dogs:

Create a Safe Space

Dogs often seek out a safe and secure place when they feel anxious or stressed. Creating a designated safe space for your dog provides them with a calming environment where they can retreat and feel protected.

- Choose a quiet area in your home, such as a corner of a room or a specific room itself.
- Set up a comfortable bed or blanket in that area, ensuring it's cozy and familiar to your dog.
- Remove any potential sources of stress or overstimulation from the space.
- Make sure the safe space is free from excessive noise, bright lights, or distractions that may contribute to anxiety.

Massage

Massaging your dog can be beneficial in releasing tension and promoting relaxation. It stimulates the production of endorphins, natural chemicals that enhance mood and overall well-being.

- Find a calm and quiet environment for the massage session, free from distractions and noises.
- Use gentle, slow strokes with your hands to massage your dog. Start with areas like the neck, shoulders, and back.
- Apply light pressure and use circular motions with your fingers or palms.
- Pay attention to your dog's response and adjust the pressure or technique accordingly.
- Massage for a few minutes, or until your dog appears relaxed and comfortable.

Aromatherapy

Specific scents can induce a calming effect on dogs by activating their olfactory receptors, which are linked to the emotional and memory centers of the brain.

- Choose a pet-safe essential oil such as lavender or chamomile, known for their calming properties.
- Dilute the essential oil with a carrier oil like coconut oil to ensure it's safe for your dog.
- Use a diffuser or spray a small amount of the diluted oil in the air in the designated area.
- Make sure the scent is not overpowering or overwhelming for your dog.
- Observe your dog's reaction to the scent and discontinue use if they show any signs of discomfort or adverse effects.

Slow, Deep Breathing

Just like in humans, slow, deep breathing can help dogs relax and regulate their nervous system. It promotes a state of calmness and can be used during anxiety-inducing situations.

- Sit or lie down next to your dog in a calm environment.
- Place your hand gently on their chest or side to feel their breathing.
- Take slow, deep breaths in and out, exaggerating the inhalation and exhalation.
- Encourage your dog to match their breathing with yours by mimicking the inhalation and exhalation patterns.

- Continue the exercise for a few minutes, or until your dog's breathing becomes slower and more relaxed.

Music and White Noise

Calming music or white noise can drown out environmental sounds and make a soothing ambiance for dogs. It can help mask sudden noises or disturbances that might trigger anxiety.

- Choose soft, calming music or white noise tracks specifically designed for dogs.
- Play the music or use a white noise machine in the designated area or wherever your dog spends most of their time.
- Adjust the volume to a level that is soothing but not overly loud.
- Allow the music or white noise to play for a period of time, especially during stressful situations or when your dog needs to relax.

TTouch Technique

TTouch is a gentle and non-invasive technique that involves circular touches, lifts, and slides on specific areas of a dog's body. These touches can help release tension, promote relaxation, and improve body awareness.

- Learn about the Tellington TTouch method from a certified TTouch practitioner, books, or online resources.
- Use gentle touches and circular motions on your dog's body, paying attention to areas of tension or sensitivity.
- Start with light pressure and adjust based on your dog's response.

- Experiment with different TTouches, such as ear slides, body wraps, or mouth strokes.
- Practice TTouch regularly to help your dog become accustomed to the technique and experience its benefits.

Calming Supplements

Calming supplements, such as natural herbs or CBD oil, can help reduce anxiety and promote relaxation in dogs. It's important to consult with a veterinarian before using any supplements to ensure they are safe and appropriate for your dog.

- Consult with your veterinarian to decide if a calming supplement is suitable for your dog's specific needs.
- Follow your veterinarian's guidance regarding the type of supplement and the recommended dosage.
- Administer the supplement as directed, whether it's in the form of treats, drops, or capsules.
- Monitor your dog's response to the supplement and consult with your veterinarian if you have any concerns or notice any adverse effects.

Calming Wrap

A calming wrap, also known as an anxiety wrap or pressure wrap, is a garment designed to provide gentle pressure to your dog's body, which can help lessen anxiety and promote relaxation.

- Purchase a calming wrap specifically designed for dogs or use a snug-fitting t-shirt or wrap that provides a gentle, even pressure.

- Place the calming wrap over your dog's torso, making sure it covers their chest and back.

- Secure the wrap snugly but not too tight. It should provide a comforting, gentle pressure without restricting movement or causing discomfort.

- Ensure the wrap is properly fitted and doesn't obstruct your dog's breathing or circulation.

- Allow your dog to wear the wrap for short periods initially to allow them to adjust to the sensation.

- Observe your dog's behavior and monitor their response to the calming wrap. Some dogs may show immediate signs of relaxation, while others may take time to adjust.

- Use the calming wrap during anxiety-inducing situations, such as during thunderstorms, fireworks, or car rides, or whenever your dog needs calming and reassurance.

- Follow the manufacturer's instructions for the specific calming wrap you're using to ensure proper usage and safety.

Note: Calming wraps can be effective for some dogs, but not all dogs respond to this technique. It's vital to monitor your dog's comfort level and consult with a professional if you have any concerns.

Exercise and Mental Stimulation

Maintaining a routine of regular exercise and providing ample mental stimulation is essential for promoting relaxation and reducing anxiety in dogs. Physical exercise helps burn off excess energy, while mental stimulation keeps their mind engaged and focused.

- Engage your dog in regular physical exercise such as walks, playtime, or interactive games.

- Provide mental stimulation through puzzle toys, treat-dispensing toys, or training sessions.

- Tailor the level and duration of exercise and mental stimulation to your dog's age, breed, and individual needs.

- Aim for a balance between physical and mental activities to prevent overstimulation and ensure your dog's overall well-being.

MONITORING AND ADAPTING MENTAL EXERCISE

Why Monitor Mental Exercise?

Monitoring mental exercise in dogs allows you to assess its effectiveness, make adjustments as needed, and ensure your dog's overall well-being. Here are some reasons why monitoring mental exercise is important:

Preventing Overstimulation: Just like physical exercise, too much mental exercise can leave a dog feeling mentally exhausted and overwhelmed. Monitoring helps prevent overstimulation and allows you to strike a balance between mental stimulation and rest.

Assessing Effectiveness: By monitoring mental exercise, you can evaluate how well it engages your dog's mind and meets their cognitive needs. This assessment helps you determine if the activities are appropriately challenging, interesting, and enjoyable for your dog.

Addressing Boredom and Behavioral Issues: Monitoring mental exercise helps identify if your dog is getting enough mental stimulation to prevent boredom. Boredom can lead to behavioral issues such as destructive chewing or excessive barking. By monitoring, you can ensure your dog is adequately engaged, reducing the likelihood of these problems.

Tracking Progress: Monitoring mental exercise allows you to track your dog's progress in cognitive tasks or training. It helps you understand your dog's strengths and weaknesses, enabling you to tailor mental exercises to their specific needs.

Signs of Effective Mental Exercise

To determine if mental exercises are effective for your dog, look for the following signs:

- Engagement: Your dog actively participates in the mental exercise, showing enthusiasm, focus, and sustained attention. They should be interested in the activity and display signs of enjoyment, such as wagging their tail or exhibiting a playful demeanor.

- Problem-Solving: Mental exercises often involve problem-solving tasks. If your dog is successfully solving puzzles, figuring out challenges, or using their problem-solving skills to complete tasks, it indicates that the mental exercise is effective.

- Mental Fatigue: After a mentally stimulating session, your dog may exhibit signs of mental fatigue, similar to how humans feel mentally tired after intense mental work. They may become calmer, seek rest, or show signs of relaxation.

- Reduced Boredom-Related Behaviors: An effective mental exercise routine should help reduce boredom-related behaviors such as excessive chewing, digging, or attention-seeking behaviors. If your dog is less prone to these behaviors, it suggests that their mental needs are being met.

Tracking Progress

Tracking the progress of your dog's mental exercises can be helpful in assessing their development, identifying areas of improvement, and staying motivated. Here are some ways to track progress in mental exercises for dogs:

- Observation: Actively observe your dog during mental exercises and take note of their behavior, responses, and improvements. Observe their problem-solving skills, memory recall, and engagement levels. Look for signs of increased confidence, efficiency in completing tasks, and overall enthusiasm during the exercises.

- Time: Keep track of the time it takes for your dog to complete certain mental exercises or tasks. As they progress, you may notice that they become faster and more efficient in solving puzzles or figuring out challenges.

- Accuracy: Monitor your dog's accuracy in completing mental exercises. Note how often they successfully solve problems or complete tasks correctly. Improved accuracy over time indicates progress in their cognitive abilities and understanding of the exercises.

- Difficulty Level: Keep a record of the difficulty level of the mental exercises you provide. Start with easier challenges and gradually increase the complexity as your dog becomes more proficient. Tracking the progression of difficulty can help you gauge their progress and ensure that they are appropriately challenged.

- Performance Metrics: Some mental exercises may have specific metrics that you can track. For example, in scent-based games, you can track the time it takes for your dog to locate hidden objects or the number of correct identifications. Having specific metrics can provide quantifiable data to measure progress over time.

- Training Journal or Diary: Maintain a training journal or diary where you can record your dog's daily mental exercises, their performance, any observations, and notable milestones. This written documentation allows you to look back and track their progress over weeks, months, or even years.

- Behavior and Engagement: Assess changes in your dog's behavior and engagement levels during mental exercises. Look for signs of increased focus, enthusiasm, and enjoyment. If you notice positive changes in their behavior and overall attitude towards mental exercises, it is a good indication of progress.

Remember that each dog progresses at their own pace, so be patient and consistent in your tracking methods. Celebrate small victories and milestones along the way. By tracking their progress, you can not only evaluate their growth but also adapt and tailor the mental exercises to their evolving needs, ensuring continued mental stimulation and development.

Adapting Mental Exercises for Dogs

Adapting mental exercises for dogs is essential to keep their minds challenged and prevent boredom. Dogs can become bored with repetitive tasks. Here are some strategies to help you adapt mental exercises for your dog:

Consider Individual Abilities and Age: Every dog is unique, and their cognitive abilities may vary. Take into account your dog's breed, age, and any physical limitations when selecting or modifying mental exercises. For example, senior dogs or dogs with mobility issues may require exercises that are less physically demanding.

Puppies and young dogs may benefit from simpler exercises that focus on basic problem-solving skills and sensory stimulation, gradually increasing the difficulty level as they grow and develop.

Start with Basic Concepts: If your dog is new to mental exercises, begin with simple concepts to build a foundation. Introduce them to basic puzzles, such as treat-dispensing toys or interactive games that require minimal problem-solving skills. As they become more comfortable and proficient, gradually introduce more complex challenges.

Gradually Increase Difficulty: Dogs, like humans, thrive on challenges. Once your dog becomes adept at basic exercises, gradually increase the difficulty level to keep them engaged and mentally stimulated. Introduce new puzzle toys, incorporate additional steps or obstacles in their games, or require them to solve more intricate problems to access rewards.

Be mindful not to overwhelm your dog. Progression should be gradual, allowing them to build confidence and master each level before moving on to the next.

Tailor Activities to Their Interests: Dogs have different preferences and interests. Pay attention to what activities your dog enjoys most, whether it's scent-based games, retrieving objects, or solving puzzles. Adapt mental exercises to align with their interests, as this will enhance their motivation and enthusiasm during the exercises.

Incorporate Variety: Keep mental exercises engaging by incorporating a variety of activities. Dogs, like humans, can become bored with repetitive tasks. Rotate different puzzles, toys, and games to provide novelty and prevent monotony. This will help maintain their interest and prevent them from losing motivation.

Combine Physical and Mental Exercise: Combining physical exercise with mental stimulation can be highly beneficial. Activities like agility training, fetch with a twist (e.g., incorporating obedience commands before each throw), or hide-and-seek with toys can provide both physical and mental exercise.

Use Positive Reinforcement: Positive reinforcement is an incredibly powerful tool when it comes to training and customizing mental exercises for dogs. Reward your dog with treats, praise, or play whenever they successfully complete an exercise or demonstrate progress. Positive reinforcement reinforces desired behavior and encourages your dog to continue engaging in mental exercises.

Modify for Special Needs or Challenges: Dogs with specific needs or challenges may require modified mental exercises. For example, if your dog has a visual impairment, you can incorporate auditory cues or scent-based games. If your dog has difficulty with physical coordination, choose puzzles that focus more on mental stimulation rather than physical dexterity.

Provide Adequate Time and Space: Mental exercises require focus and concentration. Ensure that you provide a quiet and distraction-free environment for your dog to engage in these activities. Allow sufficient time for them to explore, problem-solve, and complete the exercises at their own pace. Avoid rushing or pressuring them during the process.

Supervise and Ensure Safety: When adapting mental exercises, prioritize your dog's safety. Ensure that the puzzles, toys, or objects used are safe, free from small parts that can be swallowed or pose choking hazards. Always supervise your dog during the exercises to prevent accidents or ingestion of non-edible items.

INDOOR GAMES AND TRAINING EXERCISES

HIDE AND SEEK

Hide and Seek is an enjoyable game that engages your dog's sense of smell and problem-solving skills.

What you'll need: Treats or your dog's favorite toys.

Instructions:

1. Have your dog sit or stay in one area while you hide in another part of the house.
2. Call your dog's name and encourage them to find you.
3. When they find you, reward them with treats or praise.
4. Repeat the game by hiding in different locations.

TUG OF WAR

Tug of War is a great way to provide physical exercise and engage your dog's natural instinct to pull and tug.

What you'll need: A sturdy tug toy.

Instructions:

1. Hold one end of the tug toy and encourage your dog to grab the other end.
2. Gently tug back and forth, allowing your dog to use their strength to pull.

3. Ensure you have a good grip on the toy and maintain control of the game.
4. Use commands like "take it" and "drop it" to establish control and teach your dog proper play behavior.

DIY AGILITY COURSE

Create an indoor agility course using household items to challenge your dog's physical and mental abilities.

What you'll need: Objects like chairs, broomsticks, and blankets to set up obstacles.

Instructions:

1. Set up a tunnel using chairs and a blanket draped over them.
2. Create hurdles using broomsticks or other suitable objects.
3. Use cushions or mats for balance exercises.
4. Guide your dog through the course, encouraging them to navigate each obstacle.
5. Reward them with treats or praise for successfully completing the course.

FOOD DISPENSING TOYS

Food dispensing toys provide mental stimulation and slow down your dog's eating pace.

What you'll need: Food-dispensing toys or puzzle feeders.

Instructions:

1. Fill the food-dispensing toy with your dog's kibble or treats.
2. Give it to your dog and let them figure out how to extract the food.
3. As they manipulate the toy, small portions of food will be released, keeping them engaged and mentally stimulated.

NAME THAT TOY

This game helps your dog learn the names of their toys while engaging their memory and listening skills.

What you'll need: A variety of toys with different names.

Instructions:

1. Place a few toys in front of your dog.
2. Name one of the toys and encourage your dog to pick it up.
3. Praise and reward your dog when they select the correct toy.
4. Repeat the game with different toys and names, gradually increasing the difficulty.

SCENT WORK

Scent work taps into your dog's incredible sense of smell, providing mental stimulation and satisfaction.

What you'll need: Treats or a favorite toy, and scent-infused objects or containers.

Instructions:

1. Start by teaching your dog to associate a specific scent with a reward. For example, rub a cotton ball with a scent and reward your dog for sniffing it.
2. Place the scented object among other unscented objects or containers.
3. Encourage your dog to find the scented object by using commands like "find it" or "search."
4. Reward your dog when they correctly identify and indicate the scented object.

FLIRT POLE PLAY

Flirt poles are long poles with a rope or toy attached at one end, creating a fun game of chase for your dog.

What you'll need: A flirt pole or DIY flirt pole made from a long stick and rope.

Instructions:

1. Swing the flirt pole in circles or back and forth to simulate prey-like movements.
2. Encourage your dog to chase and grab the toy or rope attached to the pole.
3. Allow your dog to "win" occasionally by catching the toy, providing a sense of satisfaction and accomplishment.

BODY AWARENESS EXERCISES

Body awareness exercises improve your dog's coordination, balance, and spatial awareness.

What you'll need: Treats and cushions or small platforms.

Instructions:

1. Use treats to guide your dog's movement, asking them to step onto cushions or small platforms.
2. Gradually increase the difficulty by using narrower surfaces or asking your dog to balance on their hind legs.
3. Be patient and reward your dog for their efforts and progress.

MUFFIN TIN GAME

The Muffin Tin Game is a fun and mentally stimulating activity that challenges your dog's problem-solving skills.

What you'll need: A muffin tin and some treats or toys.

Instructions:

1. Place treats or toys in some of the muffin tin cups, leaving others empty.
2. Cover each cup with tennis balls or toys.
3. Inspire your dog to search for the treats by removing the balls or toys from the cups.
4. Reward your dog with the treats they find and praise their efforts.

SHELL GAME

The Shell Game is a memory-based game that encourages your dog to find hidden treats.

What you'll need: Three cups or bowls and treats.

Instructions:

1. Show your dog a treat and let them see you place it under one of the cups.
2. Shuffle the cups or bowls around, making it harder for your dog to keep track of the treat's location.
3. Encourage your dog to choose the correct cup by pawing or nudging it.
4. Be sure to reward them with a treat and offer praise to acknowledge their accomplishment.

SOCK PUPPETS

Sock Puppets is a game that engages your dog's focus and targeting skills.

What you'll need: A sock, treats, and an optional marker to draw a face on the sock.

Instructions:

1. Place a treat inside the sock and hold it closed with your hand.
2. Encourage your dog to interact with the sock puppet by pawing, nosing, or targeting it.
3. When your dog makes contact with the sock puppet, open it and let them access the treat.
4. Repeat the game, gradually increasing the difficulty by requiring more specific interactions with the sock puppet.

PUZZLE TOYS AND TREAT DISPENSERS

Puzzle toys and treat dispensers provide mental stimulation and challenge your dog's problem-solving abilities.

What you'll need: A variety of puzzle toys or treat dispensers.

Instructions:

1. Fill puzzle toys or treat dispensers with your dog's favorite treats.
2. Present the toy to your dog and encourage them to manipulate it to access the treats.
3. Different puzzle toys have varying levels of difficulty, so choose ones that suit your dog's skill level.

SIMON SAYS

Simon Says is a game that engages your dog's obedience and listening skills.

What you'll need: Treats for rewards.

Instructions:

1. Give your dog commands such as "sit," "lie down," or "shake hands."
2. Add "Simon says" before each command you want your dog to follow.
3. Reward your dog with treats for correctly following the commands given after "Simon says."
4. Vary the commands and their sequence to keep your dog engaged and challenged.

FIND YOUR TOY

Find Your Toy is a scent-based game that engages your dog's sense of smell.

What you'll need: A few of your dog's toys or treats.

Instructions:

1. Have your dog sit or stay while you place their toys or treats in various locations around the room.
2. Release your dog and encourage them to find their toys or treats using their sense of smell.
3. Be sure to reward them with a treat and offer praise when they successfully locate and retrieve each toy.

TOY CLEAN-UP

Teach your dog to tidy up their toys using positive reinforcement training.

What you'll need: A designated container or basket for toy storage.

Instructions:

1. Encourage your dog to pick up their toys one by one and place them in the designated container.
2. Use commands like "take it" and "drop it" to guide your dog's behavior.
3. Reward your dog with praise or treats for correctly placing the toys in the container.
4. Repeat the exercise regularly to reinforce the behavior and keep their play area organized.

BALLOON CHASE

Balloon Chase is a game that encourages your dog to use their paws or nose to interact with a balloon.

What you'll need: A balloon filled with air.

Instructions:

1. Gently toss the balloon in the air, encouraging your dog to chase it.
2. Allow your dog to bat the balloon with their paws or nose, keeping it in the air.
3. Celebrate your dog's successful interaction with the balloon, providing praise and encouragement.

PUZZLES WITH BOXES

Puzzles with boxes engage your dog's problem-solving abilities by hiding treats or toys inside boxes.

What you'll need: Several empty boxes of different sizes.

Instructions:

1. Place treats or toys inside one or more of the boxes.
2. Arrange the boxes in different configurations, such as stacking or hiding smaller boxes within larger ones.
3. Encourage your dog to search for the hidden treats or toys by sniffing, pawing, or opening the boxes.
4. Reward your dog with the treats or toys they find, and praise their efforts.

LASER POINTER FUN

Using a laser pointer provides mental and physical stimulation as your dog tries to catch the moving light.

What you'll need: A laser pointer.

Instructions:

1. Point the laser pointer on the floor or walls, moving it around for your dog to chase.
2. Allow your dog to "catch" the light occasionally by shining it on a treat or toy.
3. Be cautious not to shine the laser directly into your dog's eyes.

OBSTACLE COURSE

Create an indoor obstacle course to challenge your dog's physical abilities and provide a fun and engaging workout.

What you'll need: Household items such as pillows, blankets, chairs, and cones.

Instructions:

1. Set up an obstacle course using items like pillows to jump over, tunnels made from blankets, or cones to weave around.
2. Guide your dog through the course, encouraging them to complete each obstacle.
3. Reward your dog with treats or praise for successfully navigating the course.

BUBBLE CHASING

Blowing bubbles for your dog to chase is a playful and stimulating activity.

What you'll need: Bubble solution and a bubble wand.

Instructions:

1. Blow bubbles in the air, allowing your dog to chase and pop them.
2. Make sure to use a dog-safe bubble solution.
3. Encourage your dog's interaction with the bubbles, providing praise and rewards for their engagement.

FIND IT

Find It is a game that stimulates your dog's natural hunting instincts and challenges their scenting abilities.

What you'll need: Treats or toys, a towel or blanket.

Instructions:

1. Start by having your dog sit and stay in one area of the room.
2. Show them a treat or toy and let them sniff and become familiar with it.
3. Place the towel or blanket over the treat or toy, covering it completely.
4. Return to your dog and give them the command to find or search.
5. Encourage your dog to use their nose to locate the hidden treat or toy under the towel or blanket.

6. Be sure to reward them with a treat and offer praise when they successfully find the hidden item.

CUP GAME

The Cup Game challenges your dog's memory and problem-solving skills as they try to find the treat hidden under one of the cups.

What you'll need: Plastic cups, treats.

Instructions:

1. Place three plastic cups upside down in a row on the floor.
2. Show your dog a treat and let them sniff and become familiar with it.
3. Place the treat under one of the cups while your dog is watching.
4. Shuffle the cups around, mixing up their positions.
5. Encourage the dog to find the cup with the treat underneath.
6. Be sure to reward them with a treat and offer praise when they successfully choose the correct cup.

SOCK TUG-OF-WAR

Sock Tug-of-War is a fun and interactive game that channels your dog's natural instincts to tug and play.

What you'll need: Old socks.

Instructions:

1. Find a pair of old socks and tie a knot in the middle of each sock.
2. Hold one end of the sock while your dog holds the other end with their mouth.
3. Engage in a gentle game of tug-of-war, allowing your dog to pull and shake the sock.
4. Make sure to let go of the sock occasionally to give your dog a sense of victory.
5. Reward your dog with treats or praise for their participation and enthusiasm.

STAIRCASE WORKOUT

Utilize your staircase to create a challenging workout for your dog that engages their muscles and stimulates their mind.

What you'll need: Staircase, treats.

Instructions:

1. Start at the bottom of the staircase with your dog.
2. Give the command to climb the stairs and encourage your dog to follow you.
3. Once you reach the top, reward your dog with treats and praise.
4. Repeat the process, going up and down the stairs, to provide physical exercise and mental stimulation for your dog.
5. Make sure to take it at a pace suitable for your dog's fitness level and monitor their well-being throughout the activity.

TUG AND FETCH COMBO

Combine the games of tug and fetch to engage your dog physically and mentally.

What you'll need: Tug toy, ball or other fetching toy.

Instructions:

1. Start by playing a game of tug with your dog, allowing them to engage in a gentle tug-of-war with the tug toy.
2. After a few minutes of tugging, transition into a game of fetch by throwing the ball or fetching toy.
3. Encourage your dog to retrieve the toy and bring it back to you.
4. Alternate between the games of tug and fetch to keep your dog's interest and provide a well-rounded indoor exercise session.

SOCK BASKETBALL

Sock Basketball is a game that combines a love for socks and a playful game of basketball.

What you'll need: A laundry basket or box, socks, treats.

Instructions:

1. Set up a laundry basket or box as the "basket" in an open area.
2. Roll up a sock into a ball and show it to your dog.
3. Encourage your dog to pick up the sock and "shoot" it into the basket.
4. Be sure to reward them with a treat and offer praise when they successfully make a "basket."

5. Adjust the distance between your dog and the basket to increase the difficulty level.

STUFFED KONG CHALLENGE

The Stuffed Kong Challenge provides mental stimulation as your dog works to extract the treats from a stuffed Kong toy.

What you'll need: Kong toy, treats, peanut butter or wet food (optional).

Instructions:

1. Stuff the Kong toy with treats, peanut butter, or wet food.
2. Cheer your dog to work on extracting the treats from the Kong by licking and chewing.
3. You can freeze the stuffed Kong for an additional challenge and longer-lasting entertainment.
4. Be sure to reward them with a treat and offer praise when they successfully extract the treats from the Kong.

NEWSPAPER SCAVENGER HUNT

The Newspaper Scavenger Hunt game engages your dog's senses and encourages them to search for hidden treats.

What you'll need: Newspapers, treats.

Instructions:

1. Crumple up newspapers and scatter them around the room.
2. Hide treats within the crumpled newspapers.
3. Cheer your dog to search for and retrieve the treats from the newspapers.

4. Be sure to reward them with a treat and offer praise when they successfully find and retrieve the hidden treats.

SOCK PUPPET SHOW

The Sock Puppet Show is a fun and interactive game that allows you to engage with your dog using homemade sock puppets.

What you'll need: Old socks, markers or buttons (for decorating).

Instructions:

1. Take a couple of old socks and decorate them using markers or buttons to create sock puppets.
2. Put the sock puppets on your hands and engage in a playful interaction with your dog.
3. Move the sock puppets around, make them "talk," and playfully interact with your dog.
4. Reward your dog with treats or praise for their participation and enthusiasm.

SHAPE SORTING

Shape Sorting is a game that challenges your dog's problem-solving skills and their ability to match shapes.

What you'll need: Different-shaped objects (such as blocks or toys), treats.

Instructions:

1. Gather different-shaped objects and place them on the floor in front of your dog.

2. Show your dog a treat and let them sniff and become familiar with it.
3. Encourage your dog to touch or interact with a specific shape by using their paw or nose.
4. Be sure to reward them with a treat and offer praise when they successfully touch or interact with the correct shape.
5. Gradually increase the difficulty by introducing more shapes and variations.

CUPCAKE TIN PUZZLE

The Cupcake Tin Puzzle game challenges your dog to find hidden treats in a cupcake tin.

What you'll need: Cupcake tin, tennis balls or plastic cups, treats.

Instructions:

1. Place treats inside a few cups of a cupcake tin.
2. Cover the cups with tennis balls or plastic cups, mixing them up.
3. Encourage your dog to find and remove the cups or balls to access the hidden treats.
4. Be sure to reward them with a treat and offer praise when they successfully uncover and retrieve the treats.

MIRROR PLAY

Mirror Play is a game that engages your dog's curiosity as they interact with their own reflection.

What you'll need: Full-length mirror or wall-mounted mirror.

Instructions:

1. Position a full-length mirror or wall-mounted mirror in a safe area.
2. Encourage your dog to approach and interact with their reflection.
3. Playfully engage with your dog by mirroring their movements or using toys to interact with their reflection.
4. Reward your dog with treats or praise for their participation and interaction.

MUSICAL MATS

Musical Mats is a game inspired by musical chairs that challenges your dog's listening skills and impulse control.

What you'll need: Mats or small carpets, treats.

Instructions:

1. Place several mats or small carpets on the floor in a circle, one fewer than the number of participating dogs.
2. Play music or use verbal cues to encourage your dog to walk or move around the mats in a circle.
3. When the music stops or the cue is given, each dog should find a mat to sit or lie down on.
4. Remove one mat each round, and the dog left without a mat is out of the game.
5. Reward the remaining dogs with treats or praise after each round.
6. Continue playing until there is one dog left, who is the winner of the game.

TUNNEL CRAWL

Tunnel Crawl is a game that engages your dog's agility and exploration instincts as they navigate through a tunnel.

What you'll need: A dog tunnel or makeshift tunnel using blankets or chairs.

Instructions:

1. Set up a tunnel using a dog tunnel or by creating a makeshift tunnel using blankets or chairs.
2. Encourage your dog to crawl through the tunnel.
3. Be sure to reward them with a treat and offer praise when they successfully navigate through the tunnel.

NAME THAT SOUND

Name That Sound is a game that helps your dog associate specific sounds or noises with rewards.

What you'll need: Various objects that make distinct sounds, treats.

Instructions:

1. Gather objects that make distinct sounds, such as a squeaky toy, a bell, or crinkly paper.
2. Make each sound and immediately give your dog a treat.
3. Repeat the process several times, associating each sound with the reward.
4. Test your dog's response by making the sound and rewarding them when they react to it.

TARGET TRAINING

Target Training is a game that teaches your dog to touch a specific target object with their nose or paw.

What you'll need: Target stick or an object with a distinct shape or color, treats.

Instructions:

1. Show your dog the target stick or object and let them sniff and become familiar with it.
2. Present the target stick or object, and when your dog touches it with their nose or paw, reward them with a treat.
3. Gradually increase the distance between your dog and the target object, encouraging them to touch it.
4. Be sure to reward them with a treat and offer praise when they successfully touch the target object.

PLAYING WITH CHILDREN

In this section, we will explore a variety of mental exercises designed to ignite creativity, problem-solving skills, and positive interactions between dogs and children.

Engaging in activities that stimulate both your dog's mind and your children's imagination not only creates a fun and interactive environment but also strengthens the bond between them. Dogs are incredibly adaptable and social creatures, and involving them in mental exercises provides a fulfilling outlet for their energy and intelligence. These exercises not only entertain and educate your children about responsible pet ownership but also promote a sense of teamwork and cooperation between them and their furry companion.

INDOOR FETCH

This modified version of fetch can be played indoors using soft or plush toys.

What you'll need: Soft or plush toys that can be thrown safely indoors.

Instructions:

1. Teach the dog to retrieve the toy when it is thrown by a child.
2. Start by having the child toss the toy a short distance and encourage the dog to bring it back.
3. Be sure to reward them with a treat and offer praise when they successfully retrieve the toy.
4. Gradually increase the distance of the throws as the dog becomes more comfortable with the game.
5. Ensure that the game is played in a safe area, away from fragile objects or obstacles.

FIND THE TREAT

This game involves hiding treats for the dog to find with the help of the kids.

What you'll need: Treats and the participation of the kids.

Instructions:

1. Have the kids help you hide treats in various locations around the room or house.

2. Release the dog and encourage them to search for the hidden treats.
3. Once the dog finds a treat, reward them with praise and allow them to enjoy the treat.
4. Continue hiding treats in different places to keep the game challenging and engaging.

MUSICAL CHAIRS

A variation of the traditional game where the dog has to sit on a designated spot when the music stops.

What you'll need: Chairs or mats for the kids to sit on, treats, and music.

Instructions:

1. Arrange the chairs or mats in a circle, leaving one less spot than the number of participants.
2. Have the kids walk around the circle while music is playing.
3. When the music stops, the kids need to find a chair or mat to sit on, and the dog must also sit on a designated spot.
4. Reward the dog and the child sitting together with treats and praise.
5. Remove one chair or mat each round, continuing until there's only one spot left, making it more challenging.

BALLOON VOLLEYBALL

This game involves playing volleyball using a balloon, allowing the dog to interact and participate with the kids.

What you'll need: A balloon and space to move around.

Instructions:

1. Inflate the balloon and have the kids stand on one side of the room, while the dog stands on the other side.
2. Encourage the kids to gently hit the balloon over the dog's head, with the goal of keeping the balloon from touching the ground on their side.
3. The dog can use their nose or paws to keep the balloon in the air and prevent it from touching the ground on their side.
4. Reward the dog and the kids for successful volleys with treats and praise.
5. Ensure the game is played in an open area to avoid any potential accidents or damage to household items.

COPYCAT

This game involves the dog imitating the movements or actions of the kids.

What you'll need: Space to move around and the participation of the kids.

Instructions:

1. Have the kids perform simple actions such as jumping, spinning, or clapping their hands.
2. Encourage the dog to imitate the actions of the kids by jumping, spinning, or pawing the air.
3. Be sure to reward them with a treat and offer praise for successfully copying the movements of the kids.
4. Make sure the actions performed by both the kids and the dog are safe and age-appropriate.

STATUES

This game involves freezing like statues when a certain command is given, and the dog must freeze along with the kids.

What you'll need: Space to move around and the participation of the kids.

Instructions:

1. Have the kids and the dog move around the room or play area.
2. When a specific command, such as "Freeze" or "Statues," is given, everyone must freeze in their current position.
3. The dog should also freeze along with the kids and remain still until another command is given.
4. Reward the dog and the kids for successfully freezing and following the commands.
5. Vary the duration of freezing and the commands to keep the game exciting.

RING TOSS

This game involves tossing rings onto designated targets, and the dog can participate by retrieving the rings.

What you'll need: Rings (such as hula hoops) and targets (such as cones or objects).

Instructions:

1. Set up targets in different areas of the room or play area.
2. Have the kids take turns tossing the rings and aiming for the targets.
3. Encourage the dog to retrieve the rings and bring them back to the kids.

4. Reward the dog and the kids for successful ring tosses and retrieves.
5. Make sure the game is played in a safe area, away from fragile objects or obstacles.

PAW PAINTING

Paw Painting is a creative activity where your child and dog can collaborate to create unique artwork using their paws.

What you'll need: Non-toxic and washable paint, large paper or canvas, water, and towels.

Instructions:

1. Prepare the painting area by laying down the large paper or canvas.
2. Dip your dog's paw in a small amount of non-toxic paint.
3. Guide your dog's paw onto the paper or canvas to create paw prints.
4. Have your child use their hands or brushes to add additional artistic elements.
5. Repeat the process with different colors and patterns, creating a collaborative masterpiece.

SNACK TOSS

Snack Toss is a game that improves your dog's catching skills and hand-eye coordination for your child.

What you'll need: Dog-friendly treats or small toys.

Instructions:

1. Have your child stand a short distance away from your dog, holding a treat or toy.
2. Encourage your child to toss the treat or toy gently towards your dog.
3. Your dog should catch the treat or retrieve the toy in their mouth.
4. Praise and reward your dog for successfully catching or retrieving the item.
5. Gradually increase the distance and challenge your dog's catching abilities.

NAMETHAT TOY

This game involves the kids naming different toys, and the dog can fetch the correct toy based on the name given.

What you'll need: Various toys and treats.

Instructions:

1. Show the kids different toys and ask them to name each toy.
2. Teach the dog to retrieve the correct toy when the kids name it.
3. Be sure to reward them with a treat and offer praise for successfully fetching the correct toy.
4. Make sure the toys used are safe for the dog and do not have any small parts that can be swallowed.

DOGGIE BOWLING

Create a fun bowling game for your dog using plastic bottles and a soft ball.

What you'll need: Empty plastic bottles and a soft ball.

Instructions:

1. Arrange a row of empty plastic bottles and take turns with your children and dog rolling the ball to knock them down.
2. Motivate your dog to chase after the ball and express celebration or praise when they successfully topple the bottles.

CLEAN-UP RACE

Turn tidying up into a fun game by having your dog and children race to collect their toys.

What you'll need: Toys.

Instructions:

1. Scatter toys around the room and have your dog and children race to collect and put away the toys in designated bins or baskets.
2. Encourage teamwork and reward everyone's effort. This game not only helps keep the area tidy but also engages your dog's retrieval skills.

DOGGIE FASHION SHOW

Have your children dress up your dog in various outfits for a fun fashion show.

What you'll need: Dog clothes and accessories (optional).

Instructions:

1. Allow your children to select different outfits and accessories for your dog, such as hats, scarves, or vests.
2. Dress up your dog and let your children walk them down an "imaginary runway" while describing the unique features of each outfit.
3. Make it enjoyable for everyone involved and give treats or praise for their participation.

BUBBLE WRAP PARTY

Have your dog and children pop bubble wrap together.
What you'll need: Bubble wrap.

Instructions:

1. Lay out a sheet of bubble wrap on the floor.
2. Encourage your dog and children to walk on it, pop the bubbles, and have a "popping party."
3. The sound and sensation of popping bubbles can be entertaining for both your dog and children.

OUTDOOR GAMES AND TRAINING EXERCISES

FETCH

Fetch is a classic game that provides physical exercise and mental stimulation for your dog.

What you'll need: A ball or toy suitable for outdoor play.

Instructions:

1. Throw the ball or toy a moderate distance.
2. Encourage your dog to chase and retrieve it.
3. Once your dog brings back the item, reward them with praise or a treat.
4. Repeat the game by throwing the ball in different directions to keep your dog engaged.

FRISBEE

Playing Frisbee is an active game that promotes agility and coordination.

What you'll need: A Frisbee designed for dogs.

Instructions:

1. Start with short throws, gradually increasing the distance as your dog becomes more proficient.
2. Encourage your dog to catch the Frisbee in the air or after it lands.

3. Be sure to reward them with a treat and offer praise for successful catches.
4. Take breaks as needed to prevent exhaustion and overheating.

SWIMMING

Swimming is a low-impact exercise that is easy on your dog's joints and delivers a full-body workout.

What you'll need: A dog-friendly swimming area or pool, a dog life jacket (if needed), and towels.

Instructions:

1. Introduce your dog to the water gradually, allowing them to wade in and get comfortable.
2. If necessary, use a dog life jacket to ensure their safety, especially if they are new to swimming or not strong swimmers.
3. Encourage them to swim by throwing a toy or ball into the water.
4. Monitor your dog's energy level and swimming abilities, providing breaks and water as needed.

TREASURE HUNT

Treasure hunts engage your dog's scenting abilities and provide mental stimulation.

What you'll need: Treats or toys to hide and a leash (optional).

Instructions:

1. Hide treats or toys in various locations within an outdoor area.
2. If your dog is not yet trained off-leash, use a leash to guide them during the treasure hunt.
3. Encourage your dog to search for the hidden items using their nose.
4. Reward them with praise or a treat when they successfully find an item.
5. Vary the difficulty by hiding items in more challenging spots or using scent cues.

BIKE RIDING

Bike riding allows your dog to run alongside you, providing them with physical exercise and a chance to explore.

What you'll need: A bicycle, a properly fitted dog bike leash or attachment, and a safe cycling area.

Instructions:

1. Familiarize your dog with the bike and the dog bike leash or attachment.
2. Start with short and slow rides, gradually increasing the duration and speed as your dog becomes comfortable.
3. Ensure your dog is properly trained to run alongside a bike and responds to commands such as "slow," "stop," and "heel."
4. Stay alert and maintain control of the bike, ensuring the safety of both you and your dog.

DOGGY PARKOUR

Doggy Parkour involves navigating urban or natural environments with your dog, incorporating elements of climbing, jumping, and balancing.

What you'll need: A leash, treats, and an outdoor environment with suitable structures.

Instructions:

1. Explore outdoor spaces such as parks, playgrounds, or urban environments with your dog.
2. Encourage your dog to interact with different elements such as benches, logs, rocks, or stairs.
3. Be sure to reward them with a treat for successfully navigating obstacles and engaging in the environment.
4. Ensure the setting is safe and suitable for your dog's size and abilities.

DOGGY SOCCER

Doggy Soccer is a game that combines chasing and retrieving skills with the fun of soccer.

What you'll need: A soft ball suitable for your dog's size.

Instructions:

1. Set up a small goal using cones, sticks, or other markers.
2. Encourage your dog to chase and retrieve the ball, aiming to get it into the goal.
3. Be sure to reward them with a treat and offer praise when they successfully score a goal.
4. Engage in interactive play with your dog, kicking the ball and encouraging their participation.

AGILITY TUNNEL

An agility tunnel provides an opportunity for your dog to crawl through and improve their agility and confidence.

What you'll need: An agility tunnel designed for dogs.

Instructions:

1. Set up the agility tunnel in an open outdoor space.
2. Encourage your dog to enter the tunnel and crawl through it.
3. Use treats or toys to guide and motivate your dog to complete the tunnel.
4. Celebrate their success with praise and rewards.

DOGGY OBEDIENCE COURSE

Set up an outdoor obedience course to practice commands and reinforce good behavior.

What you'll need: Cones, markers, or household objects to create stations, treats, and a leash (if necessary).

Instructions:

1. Establish different stations with specific tasks or commands, such as sit, stay, lie down, or recall.
2. Guide your dog through the course, giving clear commands at each station.
3. Be sure to reward them with a treat and offer praise when they successfully complete a task.
4. Repeat the course, gradually increasing the difficulty and reinforcing obedience skills.

WATER HOSE PLAY

Playing with a water hose provides a refreshing and engaging activity for dogs, especially during hot weather.

What you'll need: A water hose with an adjustable nozzle.

Instructions:

1. Set the nozzle to a gentle spray or mist.
2. Allow your dog to chase and interact with the water as you direct the spray.
3. Be cautious not to spray water directly into your dog's face or ears.
4. Supervise your dog's play to ensure their safety and prevent them from drinking excessive amounts of water.

BUBBLE WRAP STOMP

Bubble Wrap Stomp is a sensory and interactive game that involves popping bubble wrap.

What you'll need: Sheets of bubble wrap.

Instructions:

1. Lay out the bubble wrap on the ground in an open area.
2. Encourage your dog to walk or stomp on the bubble wrap, popping the bubbles.
3. Celebrate their participation and engage in playful interactions.

SCENT WORK TRAIL

Scent work trails engage your dog's sense of smell and allow them to follow a scent trail to find hidden treats or toys.

What you'll need: Treats or toys with a scent, and a leash (optional).

Instructions:

1. Create a scent trail by placing treats or toys with a scent in various locations along a designated path.
2. If your dog is not yet trained off-leash, use a leash to guide them along the trail.
3. Encourage your dog to follow the scent, rewarding them when they find and retrieve the hidden items.

DOGGY FREESTYLE DANCE

Doggy Freestyle Dance combines obedience, tricks, and choreographed moves to create a synchronized dance routine with your dog.

What you'll need: An outdoor space with enough room for movement, treats, and music (optional).

Instructions:

1. Teach your dog various tricks and commands.
2. Create a routine that includes movements, spins, jumps, and synchronized actions between you and your dog.
3. Use treats as rewards during the training and performance.
4. Practice the routine in the outdoor space, gradually increasing the complexity and flow.

CHASE AND RECALL

Chase and Recall is a game that combines chasing and recalling commands to improve your dog's responsiveness and recall skills.

What you'll need: An open outdoor area and treats for rewards.

Instructions:

1. Allow your dog to run freely in an open area.
2. Encourage them to chase you by running in the opposite direction.
3. After a short distance, use a recall command such as "come" or "here."
4. Be sure to reward them with a treat and offer praise when they respond to the recall command and return to you.

FLYBALL

Flyball is a high-energy team sport that involves dogs racing over hurdles and triggering a ball dispenser.

What you'll need: Flyball equipment, including hurdles and a ball dispenser.

Instructions:

1. Set up the flyball equipment in an open outdoor area.
2. Teach your dog to jump over the hurdles and retrieve the ball from the dispenser.
3. Practice the sport, gradually increasing the speed and accuracy of your dog's performance.
4. Join a local flyball team or participate in competitions if available.

NATURE SCAVENGER HUNT

A nature scavenger hunt combines outdoor exploration with the challenge of finding specific items or natural elements.

What you'll need: A list of items or natural elements to find, and treats or rewards.

Instructions:

1. Create a list of specific items or natural elements for your dog to find during the scavenger hunt.
2. Take your dog to an outdoor area such as a park or nature trail.
3. Encourage them to search for the items on the list, rewarding them with treats or praise when they find each item.
4. Make sure the items are safe for your dog to interact with and avoid any toxic plants or harmful objects.

WATER RETRIEVE

Water retrieve is a game that combines swimming and retrieving skills, providing physical exercise and mental stimulation.

What you'll need: A body of water suitable for swimming, a floating toy, and towels.

Instructions:

1. Throw the floating toy into the water, encouraging your dog to swim and retrieve it.
2. Start with shorter distances and progressively increase the distance as your dog becomes more comfortable and confident.

3. Be sure to reward them with a treat and offer praise when they successfully retrieve the toy.
4. Ensure your dog's safety and monitor their energy level during the activity.

TRACKING

Tracking is an activity that taps into your dog's natural scenting abilities, requiring them to follow a scent trail to find hidden objects.

What you'll need: Treats or toys with a scent, a designated tracking area, and a leash (optional).

Instructions:

1. Create a scent trail by placing treats or toys with a scent in various locations within the designated tracking area.
2. If your dog is not yet trained off-leash, use a leash to guide them along the trail.
3. Encourage your dog to follow the scent and find the hidden items.
4. Be sure to reward them with a treat and offer praise when they successfully locate and retrieve the hidden objects.

JUMPING THROUGH HOOPS

Jumping through hoops is a fun and active exercise that can be performed outdoors.

What you'll need: Hula hoops or suitable substitutes, treats or rewards.

Instructions:

1. Set up the hula hoops or hoops of similar size in an open area.
2. Encourage your dog to jump through the hoops, starting with a low height and gradually increasing the challenge.
3. Use treats or rewards to motivate your dog and celebrate successful jumps.
4. Ensure the hoops are secure and safe for your dog to interact with.

DOGGY SOCCER GOALKEEPING

Doggy Soccer Goalkeeping involves training your dog to defend a goal while you kick a soccer ball towards it.

What you'll need: A soccer ball, cones or markers to create a goal, treats or rewards.

Instructions:

1. Set up the goal using cones or markers in an outdoor area.
2. Kick the soccer ball towards the goal, and encourage your dog to defend it by intercepting or blocking the ball.
3. Reward your dog with treats or praise for successfully defending the goal.
4. Gradually increase the difficulty by varying the speed and direction of your kicks.

CANINE DISC GOLF

Canine Disc Golf combines the game of disc golf with your dog's agility and retrieving skills.

What you'll need: Disc golf discs suitable for dogs and a disc golf course.

Instructions:

1. Choose a disc golf course suitable for both you and your dog.
2. Teach your dog to catch and retrieve the discs.
3. Throw the discs for your dog to catch while following the rules of disc golf.
4. Be sure to reward them with a treat and offer praise for successfully catching the discs.

LONG-DISTANCE WALKS

Going on long-distance walks provides your dog with physical exercise and the opportunity to explore new areas.

What you'll need: A leash, comfortable walking shoes, and water for both you and your dog.

Instructions:

1. Plan a route that offers a long and scenic walk for both you and your dog.
2. Keep your dog on a leash to ensure their safety and prevent them from wandering off.
3. Take breaks along the way for water and rest.
4. Enjoy the time spent outdoors with your dog, observing their surroundings and allowing them to sniff and explore.

DOGGY BOOT CAMP

Doggy Boot Camp combines obedience training with physical exercise to challenge your dog's mental and physical capabilities.

What you'll need: Treats or rewards and an outdoor space with enough room for training.

Instructions:

1. Create a series of obedience exercises such as sit, stay, down, heel, and recall.
2. Guide your dog through each exercise, rewarding them with treats or praise for successful completion.
3. Incorporate physical activities between obedience exercises, such as jogging or jumping.
4. Repeat the boot camp sessions regularly to reinforce obedience skills and provide a challenging workout.

SCENT DETECTION GAMES

Scent detection games engage your dog's sense of smell and provide mental stimulation.

What you'll need: Treats or toys with a scent, and an outdoor space.

Instructions:

1. Introduce your dog to the scent by allowing them to sniff and investigate the scented item.
2. Hide the scented items in various locations around the outdoor area.
3. Encourage your dog to search for and find the scented items using their nose.

4. Be sure to reward them with a treat and offer praise when they successfully locate and indicate the scented items.

FREESTYLE RUNNING

Freestyle running involves allowing your dog to run freely in an open outdoor space, providing exercise and an opportunity for them to release energy.

What you'll need: An open outdoor area, a leash (optional), and treats or rewards.

Instructions:

1. Find a secure and open outdoor space where your dog can run freely.
2. If necessary, use a leash to guide and control your dog's movements.
3. Encourage your dog to run at their own pace, exploring the area and enjoying the freedom.
4. Reward your dog with treats or praise for their active participation.

WATER SPRAY TUNNEL

Water spray tunnels provide a refreshing and stimulating activity for dogs during warm weather.

What you'll need: A hose with a nozzle that can spray a fine mist or a water sprinkler.

Instructions:

1. Set up the water spray tunnel by using a hose with a nozzle that can create a fine mist or a water sprinkler that creates a tunnel-like spray.
2. Encourage your dog to run through the water spray or play in the mist.
3. Observe your dog's comfort level and modify the water pressure to ensure they enjoy the activity.
4. Provide breaks and water if needed to prevent overheating.

BICYCLE JORING

Bicycle joring involves your dog pulling you on a bicycle, providing both physical exercise and a fun outdoor activity.

What you'll need: A dog harness or joring equipment, a bicycle, and a safe cycling area.

Instructions:

1. Familiarize your dog with the dog harness or joring equipment.
2. Attach the harness or equipment to your dog and connect it to the bicycle.
3. Start cycling at a slow and steady pace, allowing your dog to pull you.
4. Use commands such as "go," "slow," and "stop" to guide your dog's movements.
5. Observe your dog's energy level and alter the duration and intensity of the activity in view of that.

DIGGING PIT

Creating a designated digging pit provides an outlet for your dog's natural digging behavior and prevents them from digging in unwanted areas.

What you'll need: A designated area in your outdoor space, sand or soil, and toys or treats to bury.

Instructions:

1. Choose a suitable area in your outdoor space for the digging pit.
2. Fill the area with sand or soil to create a loose and diggable surface.
3. Bury toys or treats in the pit to encourage your dog's digging behavior.
4. Encourage your dog to dig in the designated area and reward them for using the pit.

FRISBEE GOLF

Frisbee golf, also known as disc golf, involves throwing frisbees into designated targets.

What you'll need: Disc golf discs suitable for dogs and a disc golf course.

Instructions:

1. Choose a disc golf course suitable for both you and your dog.
2. Teach your dog to catch and retrieve the frisbees.
3. Throw the frisbees for your dog to catch while following the rules of disc golf.

4. Be sure to reward them with a treat and offer praise for successfully catching the frisbees.

DOCK DIVING

Dock diving is a water-based sport where dogs jump off a dock into a pool or body of water.

What you'll need: A suitable dock diving location with a pool or body of water, and a floating toy.

Instructions:

1. Find a dock diving location or facility that allows dogs to participate.
2. Teach your dog to jump off the dock and into the water, retrieving a floating toy.
3. Encourage your dog to jump progressively farther distances and increase their confidence.
4. Reward your dog for successful jumps and retrieves.

CANINE FREESTYLE

Canine Freestyle combines obedience, tricks, and choreographed movements set to music, creating a synchronized dance routine with your dog.

What you'll need: An outdoor space with enough room for movement, treats, and music (optional).

Instructions:

1. Teach your dog a variety of tricks, commands, and dance movements.

2. Create a routine that includes synchronized movements, spins, jumps, and tricks between you and your dog.
3. Use treats as rewards during training and performances.
4. Practice the routine in the outdoor space, gradually increasing the complexity and flow.

SNIFF AND SEARCH

Sniff and Search games engage your dog's sense of smell and provide mental stimulation.

What you'll need: Treats or toys with a scent, and an outdoor space with hiding spots.

Instructions:
1. Show your dog a treat or toy with a scent and allow them to sniff and investigate it.
2. While your dog is distracted or in another area, hide the scented item in various hiding spots around the outdoor space.
3. Release your dog and encourage them to search for and find the hidden item using their nose.
4. Be sure to reward them with a treat and offer praise when they successfully locate and retrieve the hidden item.

DOGGY FITNESS CIRCUIT

A doggy fitness circuit involves a series of stations that target different muscle groups and provide a full-body workout.

What you'll need: Cones or markers, various exercise stations (such as sit-ups, hurdles, balance boards, etc.), treats or rewards.

Instructions:

1. Set up different exercise stations in your outdoor space, focusing on different exercises for each station.
2. Guide your dog through the circuit, encouraging them to complete each exercise at each station.
3. Reward your dog with treats or praise for successfully completing each exercise.
4. Repeat the circuit, gradually increasing the difficulty or introducing new exercises.

DOGGY LURE COURSE

A doggy lure course involves a mechanical or manual lure that your dog chases, providing a high-intensity workout.

What you'll need: A mechanical or manual lure system, an open outdoor space.

Instructions:

1. Set up the lure system at one end of the outdoor space.
2. Activate the lure, causing it to move along a predetermined path.
3. Encourage your dog to chase the lure, providing them with a vigorous workout.
4. Reward your dog with treats or praise for their participation and effort.

SOCCER DRIBBLING CHALLENGE

Soccer dribbling challenges your dog's agility and coordination as they navigate an obstacle course while keeping a soccer ball close to their paws.

What you'll need: Cones or markers, a soccer ball suitable for your dog's size.

Instructions:

1. Set up an obstacle course using cones or markers in your outdoor space.
2. Encourage your dog to dribble the soccer ball through the course, weaving in and out of the obstacles.
3. Reward your dog with treats or praise for successfully completing the course while maintaining control of the ball.
4. Adjust the difficulty level of the course as your dog becomes more proficient.

DOGGY LIMBO

Doggy limbo is a fun and flexible game that challenges your dog's flexibility and body awareness.

What you'll need: A limbo stick or a makeshift pole, treats or rewards.

Instructions:

1. Hold the limbo stick or pole at a low height and encourage your dog to limbo underneath.
2. Reward your dog with treats or praise for successfully navigating under the limbo stick without knocking it down.
3. Gradually lower the height of the limbo stick to increase the difficulty.
4. Avoid forcing your dog to bend too low if they are not comfortable.

TUG AND GO

Tug and go combines tug of war with a chase game, providing a burst of intense exercise for your dog.

What you'll need: A sturdy tug toy, treats or rewards.

Instructions:

1. Engage your dog in a game of tug of war using a sturdy tug toy.
2. After a short session of tugging, release the toy and throw it a moderate distance away.
3. Encourage your dog to chase and retrieve the toy.
4. Be sure to reward them with a treat and offer praise when they successfully retrieve the toy.
5. Repeat the game by alternating between tugging and chasing.

DOGGY OBSTACLE DASH

The doggy obstacle dash is a high-energy race through a series of obstacles designed to challenge your dog's speed and agility.

What you'll need: Cones or markers, various obstacles (such as hurdles, tunnels, weave poles), treats or rewards.

Instructions:

1. Set up a course using cones or markers and various obstacles in your outdoor space.
2. Guide your dog through the course, encouraging them to jump over hurdles, weave through poles, and go through tunnels.
3. Time your dog as they complete the course, rewarding them with treats or praise for their speed and agility.

4. Repeat the course, adjusting the difficulty and obstacles as your dog becomes more skilled.

FETCH AND HIDE

Fetch and hide combines the game of fetch with a search and find element, engaging your dog's retrieving and scenting abilities.

What you'll need: A ball or toy suitable for outdoor play, treats or rewards.

Instructions:

1. Start by playing a game of fetch with your dog, throwing the ball a moderate distance.
2. After a few rounds of fetch, hold your dog back or distract them while you hide the ball in the outdoor space.
3. Release your dog and encourage them to search for and find the hidden ball using their nose.
4. Be sure to reward them with a treat and offer praise when they successfully locate and retrieve the ball.

DOGGY TUNNEL RACE

Doggy tunnel race involves your dog racing through a tunnel as quickly as possible, testing their speed and agility.

What you'll need: An agility tunnel designed for dogs, treats or rewards.

Instructions:

1. Set up the agility tunnel in your outdoor space.

2. Encourage your dog to enter the tunnel and race through it as quickly as possible.
3. Be sure to reward them with a treat and offer praise when they successfully complete the tunnel in a fast time.
4. Repeat the race, gradually increasing the speed and challenging your dog's agility.

BOUNDARY TRAINING

Boundary training teaches your dog to stay within a designated area, providing mental stimulation and discipline.

What you'll need: Cones or markers, treats or rewards.

Instructions:

1. Set up cones or markers to create a designated boundary in your outdoor space.
2. Encourage your dog to stay within the boundary using verbal cues and rewards.
3. Gradually increase the distance or size of the boundary as your dog becomes more adept.
4. Reward your dog with treats or praise for staying within the boundary.

DOGGY BASKETBALL

Doggy basketball is a game that combines chasing, retrieving, and shooting a basketball, providing physical exercise and mental stimulation.

What you'll need: A basketball hoop suitable for your dog's size, a basketball, treats or rewards.

Instructions:

1. Set up the basketball hoop at a suitable height for your dog to interact with.
2. Encourage your dog to chase and retrieve the basketball.
3. Teach your dog to drop the basketball into the hoop or aim for the hoop with their paws.
4. Reward your dog with treats or praise for successful retrieves and shots.

DOGGY TRAMPOLINE

A doggy trampoline provides a bouncy and exhilarating exercise experience for your dog.

What you'll need: A dog-friendly trampoline or a suitable alternative, treats or rewards.

Instructions:

1. Ensure the trampoline is suitable and safe for your dog's size and weight.
2. Encourage your dog to jump and bounce on the trampoline, using treats or rewards to motivate them.
3. Observe your dog's comfort level and energy level during the activity.
4. Avoid any excessive jumping or risky behaviors that could lead to injury.

FOLLOW THE LEADER

Follow the leader is a game that encourages your dog to mimic your movements and respond to your commands.

What you'll need: An outdoor space, treats or rewards.

Instructions:

1. Start by walking or jogging around the outdoor space, with your dog following closely behind.
2. Incorporate various movements such as turning, stopping, and changing speed.
3. Use commands such as "sit," "stay," and "lie down" to test your dog's responsiveness.
4. Reward your dog with treats or praise for successfully following your movements and commands.

CANINE RELAY RACE

Canine relay races involve a team of dogs racing against each other in a relay format, providing a fun and competitive exercise experience.

What you'll need: Cones or markers, an outdoor space, multiple dogs (if available), treats or rewards.

Instructions:

1. Set up a relay course using cones or markers in your outdoor space.
2. Divide the dogs into teams and assign each team a starting point and a designated route to follow.
3. Each dog takes turns running a portion of the course and passing a baton (a toy or object) to the next team member.
4. Time the teams and reward the winning team with treats or praise.

Remember to always prioritize your dog's safety during outdoor activities. Choose activities that are suitable for your dog's size, age, and physical condition. Monitor the weather conditions to ensure your dog does not overheat or get too cold. Take breaks, provide plenty of water, and watch for any signs of fatigue or discomfort. Enjoy the time spent with your dog and have fun exploring the great outdoors together!

MENTAL STIMULATION FOR A DOG ALONE AT HOME

SNIFF AND SEEK

Sniff and Seek game engages your dog's sense of smell and provides mental stimulation.

What you'll need: Treats or toys with a scent, hiding spots (such as under rugs, inside puzzle toys, or behind furniture).

Instructions:

1. Hide treats or toys with a scent in different hiding spots around the house.
2. Encourage your dog to search for and find the hidden items using their nose.
3. Be sure to reward them with a treat and offer praise when they successfully locate and retrieve the hidden treasures.
4. Vary the difficulty by using more challenging hiding spots or adding obstacles.

INTERACTIVE FOOD TOYS

Interactive food toys provide mental stimulation and reward your dog's problem-solving efforts with tasty treats.

What you'll need: Various interactive food toys (such as treat balls, puzzle toys, or Kong toys), treats or kibble.

Instructions:

1. Fill the food toys with treats or kibble.
2. Encourage your dog to interact with the toys, figuring out how to retrieve the food.
3. Be sure to reward them with a treat and offer praise when they successfully manipulate the toys and get the treats.
4. Vary the difficulty level by using different types of interactive food toys or adjusting the size of the treats.

TREAT-DISPENSING PUZZLE TOYS

Treat-dispensing puzzle toys challenge your dog's problem-solving skills and keep them engaged.

What you'll need: Treat-dispensing puzzle toys, treats or kibble.

Instructions:

1. Fill the treat-dispensing puzzle toys with treats or kibble.
2. Show your dog how to manipulate the toys to release the treats.
3. Encourage your dog to work on the puzzles and find ways to access the treats.
4. Be sure to reward them with a treat and offer praise when they successfully solve the puzzles and get the treats.

FROZEN TREATS

Frozen treats provide mental stimulation and help keep your dog occupied for longer periods.

What you'll need: Treats, broth, ice cube trays or Kong toys.

Instructions:

1. Place treats inside ice cube trays or Kong toys.
2. Fill the trays or toys with broth and freeze them.
3. Give the frozen treats to your dog to lick and chew, providing mental stimulation and relief from boredom.
4. Monitor your dog to ensure they don't chew on the frozen treats excessively.

DIY SNUFFLE MAT

A DIY snuffle mat engages your dog's sense of smell and provides a fun and mentally stimulating activity.

What you'll need: A rubber mat or base, strips of fabric or fleece.

Instructions:

1. Cut the fabric or fleece into strips and tie them onto the rubber mat or base, creating a snuffling surface.
2. Sprinkle treats or kibble in between the fabric strips, hiding them for your dog to find.
3. Encourage your dog to search and sniff through the fabric strips to find the hidden treats.
4. Be sure to reward them with a treat and offer praise they successfully locate and retrieve the treats.

BRAIN GAMES

Brain games involve various mental challenges to keep your dog's mind engaged.

What you'll need: Treats or small toys, empty plastic bottles, muffin tins, boxes.

Instructions:

1. Use treats or small toys to create different brain games.
2. Place treats in empty plastic bottles and let your dog figure out how to get them out.
3. Hide treats in muffin tins and cover the cups with tennis balls, challenging your dog to find the treats.
4. Place treats in boxes and encourage your dog to use their paws or nose to open them and get the treats.
5. Reward your dog with treats or praise when they successfully complete each brain game.

PUZZLE TREAT TOYS

Puzzle treat toys require your dog to solve a puzzle or manipulate the toy to access the treats.

What you'll need: Puzzle treat toys (such as the Kong Classic, Nina Ottosson puzzles), treats or kibble.

Instructions:

1. Fill the puzzle treat toys with treats or kibble.
2. Show your dog how to interact with the toys to release the treats.
3. Encourage your dog to figure out how to manipulate the toys and retrieve the treats.
4. Be sure to reward them with a treat and offer praise when they successfully solve the puzzle and get the treats.

BOBBING FOR TREATS

Bobbing for treats is a fun game that challenges your dog to retrieve treats from a water-filled container.

What you'll need: A shallow container, water, treats.

Instructions:

1. Fill a shallow container with water.
2. Drop treats into the water, allowing them to sink to the bottom.
3. Encourage your dog to retrieve the treats by using their mouth or paws.
4. Be sure to reward them with a treat and offer praise when they successfully retrieve the treats from the water.

TIDY-UP TIME

Tidy-Up Time game teaches your dog to clean up their toys and provides mental stimulation.

What you'll need: A designated toy basket or box, treats.

Instructions:

1. Train your dog to associate a specific command with picking up their toys.
2. Scatter the toys around the room and give the command to clean up.
3. Encourage your dog to pick up each toy and place it in the designated toy basket or box.
4. Be sure to reward them with a treat and offer praise when they successfully clean up their toys.

SOUND PUZZLE

The sound puzzle game engages your dog's auditory sense and cognitive abilities.

What you'll need: Different objects that make distinct sounds (such as squeaky toys, rattling toys, crinkly toys), treats.

Instructions:

1. Gather different objects that make distinct sounds.
2. Place treats under a few of the objects.
3. Encourage your dog to interact with the objects and find the ones that hide the treats.
4. Be sure to reward them with a treat and offer praise when they successfully find the treats by listening to the sounds.

BALLOON FUN

Balloon Fun game engages your dog's chasing and popping instincts while providing mental stimulation.

What you'll need: Balloons, treats.

Instructions:

1. Blow up a balloon and tie a string to it.
2. Attach a treat to the string, ensuring it is securely tied.
3. Hang the balloon in a safe area for your dog to see.
4. Encourage your dog to chase and pop the balloon to retrieve the treat.
5. Be sure to reward them with a treat and offer praise when they successfully pop the balloon and get the treat.

BOX TOWER

Box Tower game stimulates your dog's problem-solving skills as they figure out how to reach the treats placed on top of a stack of boxes.

What you'll need: Sturdy cardboard boxes, treats.

Instructions:

1. Stack a few sturdy cardboard boxes on top of each other, creating a tower.
2. Place treats on top of the tower.
3. Encourage your dog to figure out how to reach the treats by knocking down or moving the boxes.
4. Be sure to reward them with a treat and offer praise when they successfully retrieve the treats from the top of the tower.

TOY SHUFFLE

Toy Shuffle game challenges your dog's memory and cognitive skills as they search for their favorite toy among a group of similar toys.

What you'll need: Your dog's favorite toy, similar-looking toys.

Instructions:

1. Show your dog their favorite toy and let them sniff and become familiar with it.
2. Introduce similar-looking toys and mix them up with the favorite toy.
3. Encourage your dog to search for and find their favorite toy among the other toys.

4. Be sure to reward them with a treat and offer praise when they successfully choose and play with their favorite toy.

SCENTED BOTTLE

Scented Bottle game engages your dog's sense of smell as they search for a hidden scented bottle.

What you'll need: A small empty plastic bottle with holes, scented cotton balls or a cloth with a strong scent, treats.

Instructions:

1. Place scented cotton balls or a cloth with a strong scent inside a small empty plastic bottle.
2. Close the bottle securely and make a few holes in it.
3. Hide the scented bottle in a room for your dog to find.
4. Encourage your dog to search for and find the scented bottle by using their nose.
5. Be sure to reward them with a treat and offer praise when they successfully locate and interact with the scented bottle.

TOY PUZZLE TOWER

Toy Puzzle Tower game challenges your dog's problem-solving skills as they figure out how to release the treats hidden in a tower of interconnected puzzle toys.

What you'll need: A variety of puzzle toys, treats.

Instructions:

1. Connect several puzzle toys together vertically, creating a tower.

2. Place treats inside the puzzle toys at different levels of the tower.
3. Encourage your dog to interact with the puzzle toys and figure out how to release the treats from each level.
4. Be sure to reward them with a treat and offer praise when they successfully solve the puzzle and retrieve the treats.

CONCLUSION

Mental exercises play a crucial role in keeping dogs stimulated, engaged, and mentally sharp. They provide a valuable outlet for their natural instincts, intelligence, and problem-solving skills. Engaging in mental exercises can help prevent boredom, alleviate anxiety, and promote overall well-being in dogs.

By incorporating mental exercises into your dog's routine, you can provide them with a healthy outlet for their energy and mental stimulation, especially when they are alone at home. These activities can range from simple games that challenge their senses, memory, and problem-solving abilities to interactive toys and puzzles that keep their minds actively engaged.

Not only do mental exercises provide entertainment for your dog, but they also strengthen the bond between you and your furry friend. The time spent engaging in these activities allows for positive interactions, communication, and mutual understanding. It is an opportunity for you to observe and appreciate your dog's intelligence, adaptability, and unique personality.

So, why not give mental exercises a try? Experiment with different games, toys, and puzzles to find what captivates and challenges your dog the most. Remember to start with activities suitable for your dog's age, abilities, and preferences, gradually increasing the difficulty level as they become more proficient.

Encourage your dog, provide them with positive reinforcement, and celebrate their achievements during these mental exercises.

The joy and satisfaction they experience when they successfully solve a puzzle or find a hidden treat will be evident in their wagging tail and bright eyes.

Embrace the power of mental stimulation and make it a part of your dog's daily routine. Not only will you be helping them lead a happier and healthier life, but you will also create a deeper and more fulfilling bond with your canine companion. So, let the mental exercises begin and enjoy the wonderful journey of discovery and enrichment with your beloved dog!